Another Way to Be

Another Way to Be

SELECTED WORKS OF

Rosario Castellanos

EDITED AND TRANSLATED BY

MYRALYN F. ALLGOOD

Foreword by Edward D. Terry

The University of Georgia Press   Athens & London

© 1990 by the University of Georgia Press
Athens, Georgia 30602
All rights reserved
Designed by Richard Hendel
Set in Berkeley
The paper in this book meets the guidelines
for permanence and durability of the
Committee on Production Guidelines for
Book Longevity of the Council on Library
Resources.

Printed in the United States of America
94 93 92 91 90   5 4 3 2 1

Library of Congress
Cataloging in Publication Data
Castellanos, Rosario.
  [Selections. English. 1990]
  Another way to be : selected works of
Rosario Castellanos / edited and translated by
Myralyn F. Allgood ; foreword by Edward D.
Terry.
     p.   cm.
  Selections translated from the Spanish.
  Includes bibliographical references.
  ISBN 0-8203-1222-3 (alk. paper)
  ISBN 0-8203-1240-1 (pbk.: alk. paper)
  1. Castellanos, Rosario—Translations,
English.   I. Allgood, Myralyn Frizzelle.
II. Title.
PQ7297.C2596A22   1990
861—dc20   89-20530
                    CIP

British Library Cataloging in
Publication Data available

To the memory of

ROSARIO CASTELLANOS

There must be another way. . . .

Another way to be human and free.

Another way to be.

　　—Rosario Castellanos,

　　　"Meditación en el umbral"

Contents

Foreword *by Edward D. Terry*   xi

Preface   xv

Acknowledgments   xix

INTRODUCTION
Rosario Castellanos: Eminent Example of the
New Mexican Woman   xxi

POETRY

Apuntes para una declaración de fe / Notes for a Declaration of Faith	6
Muro de lamentaciones / Wailing Wall	8
Baño ritual en el Grijalva / Ritual Bath in the Grijalva	10
Lavanderas del Grijalva / Washerwomen on the Grijalva	12
La oración del indio / The Indian's Prayer	14
Madre india / Indian Mother	16
Una palmera / A Palm Tree	20
Misterios gozosos / Joyful Mysteries	22
La velada del sapo / The Frog's Soirée	24
Revelación / Revelation	26
Nacimiento / Birth	28
Lívida luz / Livid Light	30
Presencia / Presence	32
Memorial de Tlatelolco / Tlatelolco Memorial	34

PROSE FICTION

Three Knots in the Net	44
From *Balún-Canán* (The Nine Guardians)	59
The Luck of Teodoro Méndez Acúbal	70

The Cycle of Hunger   76
From *Oficio de tinieblas* (Tenebrae Service)   97
Cooking Lesson   104

ESSAYS

In Praise of Friendship   116
Man of Destiny   119
Women's Lib, Here   122
Genesis of an Ambassador   125
A World of Change   128
Sheer Diplomacy   131

Notes   135

Selected Bibliography   139

Foreword

The writings of Rosario Castellanos are imbued with the spirit of Chiapas, her *patria chica*. To peruse them is to become acquainted with that region, as one does the Valley of the Cauca in Colombia by reading Jorge Isaacs's *María*. Although I had seen the regional dance "Las Chiapanecas" in Morelia, Michoacán, as a young undergraduate student, it was not until June 1980 that I was able to visit Chiapas. Another Chiapanecan writer, Oscar Palacios, extended the invitation and showed me San Cristóbal de las Casas, San Juan Chamula, and other historic and beautiful areas of Mexico's southernmost state.

The climate and geography of Chiapas is varied, ranging from the steamy jungle area of Palenque to the cool highlands of San Cristóbal and Comitán to Tapachula on the tropical Pacific coast. The state has beautiful lakes and luxuriant forests and mountains with stately pines that remind me of certain parts of Alabama and the southeastern United States. Chiapas is an area that differs sharply from arid Yucatán to the east—also home of the Maya—and the barren areas of northern Mexico. It is a land of contrasts, of poetry, and of solitude, all of which Rosario Castellanos infuses into her literature.

A few years ago I had the opportunity to work with Professor Myralyn Allgood on her dissertation, which dealt with the indigenist fiction of Rosario Castellanos. For this reason, it was a special pleasure for me to be asked to write the foreword to this collection of Castellanos's translated works. Professor Allgood is knowledgeable not only of the author but also of Chiapas. Consequently, she was able to locate obscure material and contact individuals close to "Rosario, La Chiapaneca."

Professor Allgood has made excellent selections for her translations from Castellanos's varied writings, examples that will give the public a taste of the themes of solitude, of despair, and of hope that appear in her works. Well before her tragic death in August of 1974, Castellanos had been recognized by critics as an important young writer with "a new voice." The recipient of many awards and recognitions, she was named Mexico's Woman of the Year in 1967. In 1971 President Luis Echeverría appointed her ambassador to Israel, and later bestowed on her the additional honor of the coveted Sourasky Prize for Literature.

Rosario Castellanos's initial literary efforts were in poetry, for which she felt a calling the rest of her life. In some of her lyrics there are traces of the influence of the Chilean Nobel laureate Gabriela Mistral, whom she, of course, admired: anguish, despair, and a love for nature and for children. Other themes are a search for identity and social justice for the Indian. The poem "Madre india" is an excellent example of her empathy and compassion for the natives of Chiapas. Castellanos paints a poignant image of their struggle against hunger, poverty, and humiliation. She harshly condemns the Ladino (white man) for the centuries-old abuse of having usurped the Indians' patrimony, and displays with vibrant emotion her profound sense of outrage over their mistreatment. This is a topic she deals with more at length in her indigenist prose fiction. Castellanos's poetry also served as a catharsis for the anguish and despair in her own life.

Chiapas's geographical isolation conspired with the hacienda owners to prevent the full implementation of the Revolution of 1910, until President Lázaro Cárdenas initiated land reform there in the 1930s. Rosario Castellanos had been a lonely, rejected child while growing up in Chiapas. Thanks to her Indian *nana,* she was able to penetrate gradually the natives' world of superstition, myth, and humiliation by the Ladino. In so doing, she came to appreciate the value of their rich cultural heritage, even though it was different from her own.

In her indigenist prose fiction, Castellanos gives a different view of the Indians from that portrayed by the earlier *indigenista* novelists such as Gregorio López y Fuentes of Mexico, Jorge Icaza of Ecuador, and Ciro Alegría of Peru. She perceives them from within their culture, and sees them as human beings instead of mass personages or stereotypes. Castellanos analyzes the conflicts between Indians and Ladinos and among the individuals of both groups, thereby emphasizing the time warp of that provincial world that is characterized by the superstition and myth of the native and by the reality of the white. Time had stood still, stagnated, for the Indian since the Conquest, in that the abuses continued much the same in the twentieth century as they had in the sixteenth.

By use of such modern literary techniques as interior monologue, indirect discourse, and flashbacks, Rosario Castellanos creates well-rounded, realistic characters, both Ladino and Indian. Consequently, she also shows what might be considered the Indians' unfavorable side: deep-rooted superstition, occasional alcoholism, and the demeaning effects of centuries-old humiliation by the white master. Nevertheless, Castellanos compassionately portrays the positive and the human side of the Indians, with hope for their future expressed through their determination to survive. Thus she has helped remove the past masks of stereotype and idealization and has placed the Indians in the present moment, along with the problems created by four centuries of abuse.

She brings out the universal aspects of their nature, of human nature, in a provincial society. Without a doubt, the *nana* and other Indians of her childhood were a predominant influence in Castellanos's perception of a reality that the hacienda owners' children rarely saw.

Later in her theater and her essays we see the final stages in Rosario Castellanos's literary evolution from loneliness and melancholy to an expression of wit and humor. She recalls a sardonic Sor Juana Inés de la Cruz as "La Chiapaneca" satirizes the ridiculous idea that women might begin to think—an evil that must be avoided at all costs. Continuing in the same vein, she pokes fun at the traditional role of the Mexican wife and the traditional values of her society.

In one essay, departing from Aristotle, Castellanos reveals her inner self in an analysis of friendship. In another, she ironically refers to Lázaro Cárdenas, who caused her family's world to collapse, as a "man of destiny" and thanks him for affording her more opportunities than the traditional ones for a woman. (At this point we might wonder how Sor Juana would have fared if such a "man of destiny" had existed in the seventeenth century.)

Castellanos also comments on the changing social conditions in Mexico and the feminist movement in the United States around 1970. At another time she nostalgically meditates on how the world has changed since her son Gabriel was three years old. In possibly her last essay, written in August 1974, when she was ambassador to Israel, Castellanos discusses diplomacy with satirical humor, again showing the evolution of her disposition and style.

Rosario Castellanos's sense of justice and fair play, her compassion for the Indian and all oppressed, and the quality of her literary works gained respect and affection for her among her contemporaries. Professor Allgood provides a valuable contribution to a greater understanding of "Rosario, La Chiapaneca" by making this collection available to the general public.

Edward D. Terry, Professor of Spanish
Director, Alfredo Barrera Vásquez Center for Yucatecan Studies
The University of Alabama

Preface

I was first introduced to the works of Rosario Castellanos as a graduate exchange student in the School of Philosophy and Letters of the National Autonomous University of Mexico. My professor of Mexican literature was María del Carmen Millán, a respected writer and critic and the first woman to be inducted into the Academia Mexicana de la Lengua. A colleague and close personal friend of Castellanos to whom the author dedicated her essay collection *El mar y sus pescaditos* (The Sea and Its Little Fishes), Dr. Millán shared with her students the admiration she felt for Rosario's outstanding personal and literary qualities, which she described as "intense brilliance, tireless commitment, a constant search for perfection, generous human kindness, and singular wit."

Since those days, I have followed with interest the unfolding of Castellanos's literary career and have come to respect the talent and dedication with which this remarkable woman filled her multiple roles of writer, teacher, homemaker, and diplomat.

Today, fifteen years after her untimely death in 1974, Castellanos is considered one of Mexico's most distinguished literary personalities, "the writer who has portrayed the problems of the Indians with the greatest depth" (Millán), and is admired not only for her abilities as poet, essayist, short story writer, novelist, and critic, but also for the warmth of her personality and for the breadth and quality of the sum total of her cultural and human achievements.

In view of the esteem in which she is held in her own country, it is surprising that so little investigative work has been done on Rosario Castellanos's life and literary production. While reviews of her poetry are abundant, analysis of her short stories is scant, and criticism regarding her novels deals mainly with indigenist and feminist themes. Even less work has been done on her plays and essays. As for translation, only one of her novels has been rendered in English, and it is no longer in print. Several of her poems have been translated, along with a few short stories and essays, one play, and a fragment of her second novel. Biographical material is scant—perhaps because she was such a well-known figure to Mexican readers—and practically none is available in English.

Because her work is of such significance and because she has so much to say to readers everywhere, I feel that a collection such as the present volume is long overdue. It is time that the English-speaking public had an opportunity to experience the work of this versatile and dedicated writer.

I have attempted to gather selections that are representative of the many facets of the Castellanos canon. Immediately following my introductory essay is a bilingual section of her earliest and most prolific genre, poetry. Included there is a previously unpublished poem written in 1948 and an undated prose poem seen in print only once, in a local newspaper, on the first anniversary of her death. After the poetry comes a collection of her prose works—four short stories and excerpts from the two novels. These, in turn, are followed by a group of her essays and a selected bibliography.

Appreciation is due numerous persons who, in their several ways, played a vital role in the progress of this project. Special thanks go to Francisco Márquez Páez, Octavio Gordillo Ortiz, and the staffs of the National Library and the Periodical Library in Mexico City for their helpful suggestions and invaluable assistance that led to the location of many unforeseen sources of data. I am greatly indebted to the hospitality of Oscar, Hilda, and Marta Palacios of Tuxtla Gutiérrez and to the friends and colleagues of Rosario Castellanos in Chiapas who so graciously gave of their time to share bits of information and personal insights into her life and works: Armando Duvalier of the Institute of Arts and Sciences of Chiapas in Tuxtla Gutiérrez; Armando Aguirre, resident anthropologist for the Tzeltal-Tzotzil Coordinating Center of the National Indian Institute in San Cristóbal de las Casas; and Oscar Bonifaz of Comitán, writer, Director of Education and Artistic and Cultural Promotion of Chiapas, and newly appointed director of the Rosario Castellanos Museum in Tuxtla Gutiérrez.

I am especially indebted to Professor Bonifaz for his friendship and encouragement and for sharing with me and our readers the lovely little poem Rosario gave him so many years ago. His knowledge of Chiapas and his close association with the Castellanos family have provided me with many valuable insights, and I am deeply grateful. I also wish to express my appreciation to Gabriel Guerra Castellanos, Rosario's son and literary heir, for his enthusiastic collaboration in this volume and for permission to reproduce and translate his mother's works, and to Fondo de Cultura Económica for permission to reprint the poems from *Poesía no eres tú*.

My gratitude is also extended to Lynn Buttemere, Laurie Geiger, and Lorna Ables for their assistance with preliminary drafts; and again to Lorna, along with Mary Weiss, Rossana Saenz, Lara Smith, and Lynda Reynolds, for their expert typing of the text; and to my dear friends Grace and Francisco Márquez,

Janice Lasseter, and my mother, Sybil Frizzelle, for their critical reading of the manuscript, which has resulted in many significant improvements of the text.

I also wish to express my appreciation to Elizabeth Makowski and Karen Orchard of the University of Georgia Press for their interest and encouragement throughout the evolution of this project, to Ed Terry for his orientation and guidance in the early stages of my research, to Samford University for grants to assist in preparing the manuscript, to my patient and understanding family for a lifetime of love and confidence, and to my colleague Charlotte Coleman for her cheerful and enthusiastic company on my trek through Chiapas.

Finally, and most of all, I must thank Rosario herself, for her genius, for the continuing inspiration of her life, for her commitment to integrity and her search for justice and dignity. I find in her a kindred soul and have felt her guiding spirit close at hand during the months and years of research and writing.

It is my firm hope that those who read this collection of her works will experience the warmth and genuine affection that come through the pages of her writings. I have attempted to let Rosario speak for herself—through the self-revealing statements in her poetry and essays and the many interviews she so graciously granted—joining her voice with mine and the many others who have analyzed and commented on her works over the years.

Myralyn F. Allgood

Acknowledgments

The editor wishes to thank the following Mexican publishers for the use of their Spanish texts from which the translations were taken:

Editores Mexicanos Unidos for *El uso de la palabra*.

Editorial Joaquín Mortiz for *Album de familia* and *Oficio de tinieblas*.

El Sol de Chiapas for "Madre india."

Fondo de Cultura Económica for *Poesía no eres tú* and *Balún-Canán*.

Universidad Veracruzana for *Ciudad Real*.

Secretaría de Educación y Cultura del Gobierno del Estado de Chiapas for "Tres nudos en la red."

Fellowman, wherever you are,
wherever you live,
there shall we all remain.
　　—Rosario Castellanos, "Presencia"

. . . of myself and of Him
and of us three, always three!
　　—José Gorostiza, Muerte sin fin

Rosario: Voice of the Mountain, Earth, Anger, and Hope
　　—Dos Puntos: Periódico de la República en Chiapas

But if we walk in the light . . . we have fellowship one with another.
　　—1 John 1:7

Rosario Castellanos

Eminent Example of the New Mexican Woman

Among the voices that spoke out in tribute to Rosario Castellanos at the time of her tragic death in 1974 was that of Mexico's premier poet, Carlos Pellicer:

Rosario Castellanos is an eminent example of the new Mexican woman. An admirable poet and short story writer, a novelist who portrays the situation of the Indians of Chiapas so miserably treated since the first moments of the Conquest, her love for exploited human beings, her progressive ideas, her work as professor at the National University, her labors as Mexican Ambassador to Israel, her goodness, her moral integrity—all made of Rosario Castellanos, whose recent loss in the plenitude of life we her admirers so profoundly lament, an eminent example of the new Mexican woman. [1]

The years since her death have witnessed a renewed appreciation of Rosario Castellanos's many contributions to Mexican life and an enhanced awareness of the artistic merit of her multifaceted creative endeavors. Beloved as one of her country's most distinguished literary personalities, she is an insightful and ironic interpreter of Mexico's cultural uniqueness.

Portraying in her works the reality she viewed from her vantage point as "Mexican and woman," [2] she brought to light the social codes that reigned in the tradition-bound communities where Indians were abused and exploited and women were condemned to lives of self-abnegation and submission. With both sadness and humor, she denounced the pervasive injustice that required society's weaker members to sacrifice their own needs and aspirations to the demands of their stronger counterparts.

In her works, interracial and interpersonal relationships fall into patterns of dominator and dominated, but the characters are all individuals—lifelike fictional beings with both virtues and vices, who struggle to establish their own identities within an often hostile environment. There are often tragic consequences for such assertive action, but in the very struggle is seen a glimmer of hope for a remedy to this "vicious circle that must be broken."[3]

Rosario, La Chiapaneca

Rosario Castellanos derived her concept of injustice not so much from metaphysical ponderings as from the realities of the life she experienced from her childhood onward. Born in Mexico City in 1925, she spent her early years in the remote state of Chiapas, traveling back and forth between the town of Comitán de las Flores near the Guatemalan border, and the Hacienda de El Rosario, which was part of her father's extensive landholdings. On these trips she, her mother, and her younger brother were carried in hand-chairs under a canopy that the Indians carried over their heads. To her these Mayan-speaking Indians in Chiapas were no more than "a part of the landscape,"[4] and being attended by them in all daily activities was a way of life simply taken for granted. Through the years she witnessed many acts of cruelty and injustice and many abuses of the semi-feudal latifundio system, and as she grew older, her conscience and sense of human dignity caused her to reject that way of life. She gave the lands she had inherited to the Indians who worked them and went to work for the National Indian Institute in San Cristóbal de las Casas.

This Chiapas where Castellanos spent so much of her life, far from the heart of Mexico and almost totally isolated from the rest of the country, remained in her day very much like the conquistadors found it centuries before.

When the Spaniards first arrived in Teochapan, the ancient name for Chiapas, they discovered a lush tropical land inhabited by a number of indigenous groups of Mayan descent: Tzotzil, Tzeltal, Tojolabal, Zoque, Maya-Lacandón, and others. Though the first encounter between Spaniard and Indian was peaceful, the Spaniard's insatiable desire for gold and other tributes led to numerous Indian rebellions that were ultimately crushed by Spanish forces. In 1528 the town of Ciudad Real (today San Cristóbal de las Casas) was founded. During the colonial period, Dominican and Mercedarian missionaries undertook the task of evangelizing the natives, the chief among these churchmen being Fray Bartolomé de las Casas. Named first bishop of Chiapas in 1545, he lived and worked in the city that today bears his name, where he labored tirelessly in defense of the Indians and against the abusive encomienda system that kept them enslaved.

In spite of his efforts, the subjugation of the local people continued, but not without periodic uprisings that took a high toll of lives on both sides.

One of these Indian rebellions serves as the historical background for Castellanos's novel, *Oficio de tinieblas* (Tenebrae Service), although the time frame was shifted from the mid-nineteenth century of its actual occurrence to the early-twentieth-century presidency of Lázaro Cárdenas, the era of her youth and the time when changes were beginning to take place in Chiapas.

When Cárdenas came to power in 1934, he was committed to the task of carrying out the Agrarian Reform programs that began as a result of the Mexican Revolution of 1910. By 1940 he had distributed nearly forty-five million acres of hacienda lands into communal plots, or ejidos, so that, at last, the Indians had land of their own.

In efforts to free his countrymen from oppression and to bring marginal groups into the mainstream of Mexican life, Cárdenas put into effect numerous other social reform programs. He encouraged the organization of farm cooperatives and worked to bring educational opportunities into even the most remote areas of the country. Referred to as an "unconditional feminist," he was also determined to see women incorporated into the productive economic life of the country and supported the organization of women's groups, educational and legal equality for women, as well as their right to vote.[5] These changes were all taking place, in Chiapas and elsewhere, during the formative years of Rosario Castellanos, who later wrote about their effect on her and her community:

As was our custom, we were living in Comitán. It was that heroic time when General Cárdenas was trying to divide up the large estates to implement Agrarian Reform in an area where such a policy was considered impractical and harmful. I remember lingering in hallways and patios—where I was supposed to be playing—to listen to the conversations of my parents and their friends, all owners of vast expanses of land, cattle, and coffee plantations. They were impassioned conversations, interspersed with curses for a government that was taking the country ("the country," of course, meant them, not those ignorant and foul-smelling Indians on whom they were trying to confer a degree of personal dignity, and even worse, landownership) down the road to chaos and ruin.[6]

As this passage indicates, Cárdenas's zeal for social change was not shared by the Ladino (the term used in Chiapas for non-Indians) inhabitants of the area, who were reluctant to relinquish their traditional position of privilege. The Indians, for their part, had been convinced by presidential oratory that they had rights equal to any white man and became restless and desirous to see this ideal become reality. Thus is set in motion the interracial conflict that serves as background for *Balún-Canán* (The Nine Guardians), *Ciudad Real* (Royal City), and *Oficio de tinieblas* (Tenebrae Service). Similar conflicts based on changes in the traditional views of women's role in society, also stemming from this period, appear as early as these three books of Indian theme and are the focus of Castellanos's later works.

The old patterns of dominator and dominated, whether in Ladino/Indian or male/female relationships, were hard to break, particularly in an area isolated both physically and spiritually from the urban population centers of the central portion of the country. Thus Chiapas remained an island of prejudice and discrimination in the midst of a changing world.

The Cycle of Chiapas: The Indigenist Novel

Rosario Castellanos is credited with "bringing to its culmination point a new approach to the treatment of the Indian in the Mexican novel."[7] In an interview she delineated the Indians' important role in Mexican history and explained why she and many of her fellow writers have felt compelled to write about these native Americans in their novels and stories:

From the perspective of our ivory tower, the Indian is like the air: invisible but omnipotent. In fact . . . he has been the most active and effective protagonist in our history. The Indian is, after all, the point of reference by which the mestizo is mestizo, and the Creole and white so important, because they compare themselves with someone whom they relegate to the lowest possible human category. Or they are impertinently generous, conferring upon someone infinitely more deprived than they the possibility of becoming their equal. Who, but the Indian peon . . . created, with his labor, the fineries enjoyed by the privileged classes? . . . Who believed, until death, in our quixotic revolutions? Who bore, with silent stoicism, the exploited hopes, the unfulfilled promises made by popular leaders who in the end betrayed his interests for those of an oligarchy? Such facts are ever present, directly or indirectly, in each of our consciences, our memories, and our projects. When we write, such ideas rush to the fore.[8]

Rather than the "noble savage" of the Romantic period, or the stereotyped victim in the later *indigenista* novels of social protest, the novels of Castellanos's generation of writers turned to the quest for identity for the Indians through a closer examination of their way of life, their mythology, and their role in history. These novels include, in addition to Castellanos's, the works of Ricardo Pozas, Ramón Rubín, Francisco Rojas González, Eraclio Zepeda, and Carlo Antonio Castro, and take place principally in Chiapas, home to one of the highest concentrations of Indians of any area of Mexico.

These works, termed "The Cycle of Chiapas" by Joseph Sommers, the preeminent scholar on indigenist themes in Castellanos's works, are inspired by narrative-type works of an anthropological nature. While they have much in common with their immediate predecessors—the novels of B. Traven—these new novels and stories take a different point of departure and focus more closely on the Indians themselves, seen within their own cultural context. Here, for the first time, the reader comes in contact with convincing Indian characters, pictured in their own specific environment, and with authentic personalities. The pervading theme is the anguish that these characters suffer as they live out their lives in the midst of the difficult physical and social circumstances that prevail in their native Chiapas.

These authors attempt to penetrate the psychology and cosmology of the Indians and to demonstrate how their particular mythical concepts influence their way of thinking and, thereby, their behavior. Most combine anthropology and literary elements to produce works that have merit not only as social documents but as enduring human narratives as well. The common thread that runs through all is the influence of such indigenous concepts as legends, mythical symbolism, the role of the supernatural in daily life, and the Indian notion of circular time. Guided by their own artistic philosophies and the prevailing literary current of their times, these authors remain primarily realists, but with a new, profoundly personal and individualized realism. Their concern for the personal anguish of their protagonists brings them into common bond with other postwar writers who also chronicle the universal human condition of sadness and suffering. Using the Chiapanecan Indian as their point of departure, they have created novels of synthesis that bring together elements of past and present and that treat themes both regional and universal.

These new trends find an ideal exponent in Rosario Castellanos. Reared in the midst of the Tzotzil-Tzeltal cultures and having returned as an adult to do social work there, she had experienced the Indian way of life at first hand. Her privileged perspective brings added depth and substance to the Cycle of Chiapas as she strives to affirm the dignity and human value of the Indian in each of her works. She explores the conflicts and dilemmas that color his existence, removing the idealizations and stereotypes of the past and providing a convincing presentation of the Indian as a fellow being who has an important role to play in Mexican daily life: "An Indian is, essentially, a man whose development could have been affected, positively or adversely, by his circumstances. His adversity should not infer any blame on his part, nor should it justify any abusive forms of treatment. Mestizos and whites will be surprised to find in him (that 'someone else' who has never even attained classification beyond that of a 'thing') a fellow human being, an interlocutor, even a possible competitor" (*El uso,* 167).

For this reason, she disagrees with the critics who include her as a traditional *indigenista:*

Critics have generally chosen to include me within the indigenist current because the characters in most of my books are Indians, or Mestizos, or whites seen in relation to their Indian counterparts. However, I do not feel that such a classification is valid, since what is generally understood to be indigenist literature is characterized by a series of stereotypes, a Manichean concept of the world, in which the "good guys" and the "bad guys" are designated by the color of their skin. And, naturally, the "good guys" are the Indians because they are the victims, and the "bad guys" are the whites because they have power, authority, and money. I simply do not believe these patterns to be correct. Precisely what I have tried to do in all my books is prove those assumptions false, so that the essential ambiguity of the human being might come to light—along with the series of contradictions that prevails in all social relationships. . . . I feel that this has been the great error of all the *indigenista* writers up to now, that is, the belief that the Indian is like a creature from outer space. Only when we are able to view him as a human being can we make him a true literary personage. [9]

In her attempt to create literary personages who are also convincing human beings, Castellanos has created her own unique style, which juxtaposes traditional realism with more innovative narrative expressions. In order that the stories' content and the characters' conduct may be clearly understood, she prefers a simple, straightforward way of writing: "The story is, in and of itself, complicated and confusing enough without adding to it architectural and artistic difficulties." [10] In analyzing the underlying drives and emotional states of her personages, however, she adds a significant amount of flashback and thought presentation. In this way, she is able to offer her readers an overview of several sets of realities and relationships, thereby creating believable individual characters, Indian and Ladino alike, as she endeavors to present the broader panorama of Chiapanecan life.

Characters

In analyzing Rosario Castellanos's works, Margarita García Flores made the following observation: "Other writers are concerned mainly with God, or nature, or objects. Rosario Castellanos, on the other hand, was most interested in human relationships." [11]

As a result of this strong interest, Rosario Castellanos places the focus of her literary narrative on the development of characters and their interaction with one another. She sees her personages as important in themselves, not merely as the products of economic and political forces, and goes to great lengths to portray their inner psychology as they react to their own circumstances and relationships.

Her emphasis on the inner worlds of both Indian and Ladino corresponds to her view of the individual as a multifaceted being, a creature with both good and evil qualities. "At first glance one has the impression that the role of victim should be the Indian's and the white man's that of victimizer," she observes. "But human relationships are not that systematic, and those of society in general even less so. Sometimes the masks are exchanged, the roles reversed" (*Juicios,* 125–26).

She goes on to explain: "Indians are human beings no different from whites. They simply live in very different—and unfavorable—circumstances. Since they are weaker, they have more potential for evil—violence, treachery, and hypocrisy—than whites. I do not find Indians to be either mysterious or poetic. What is a fact is that they live in atrocious misery. We must show how that misery has atrophied their best qualities."[12]

As for the Ladinos, they, too, have both positive and negative character traits, and, like any other human beings, are capable of victimizing those who are weaker. They do not do so, however, with impunity, for in mistreating others they too suffer the dehumanization that this role brings with it. "The sword of injustice," as Castellanos quotes Simone Weil, "is a two-edged sword that wounds the one who wields it just as brutally as it does its intended victim" (*Juicios,* 126).

All of Rosario Castellanos's characters, whether Indian or Ladino, male or female, are individuals with weaknesses and strengths, vices and virtues, wants and needs. They emerge as unique entities, with their own identities and personalities, and their own peculiar relationship to each other and to their environment. While their interpersonal relationships tend to fall into patterns of dominator and dominated, all are victims of one sort or another—of a suffocating environment, a tyrannical *patrón,* an inherited mythology, a decadent society, an unresponsive spouse, or an unresolvable psychological conflict within the characters themselves.

Perhaps one of the reasons Castellanos was so successful in creating lifelike characters is that most were actually taken from life. These individuals, their situations, and their conflicts are authentic—remembered, understood, and recorded from the author's own experiences. Her Indian nursemaid, or *nana,* and the workers on her father's ranch, along with such memorable events as the death of her brother, the problems of an uncle or a neighbor, and a cousin lured into the mountains by evil spirits all find their way into the pages of her literary creation.

In response to questions about her well-developed female characters, Castellanos stated that they, too, were patterned after people she knew. She went on to explain that their portrayal as literary figures satisfied her own personal need to breach human solitude and to create a sense of solidarity with other women:

Even my most distant memories are rooted in personal solitude. And I soon discovered that all the women I knew found themselves in the same condition: lonely spinsters, lonely wives, lonely mothers. Lonely, enduring the most rigid of customs that condemned love and surrender as mortal sins. Lonely in their idleness, because that was the only luxury they could afford. Portraying these lives, delineating these characters has resulted in a creative process that is primarily autobiographical. I escaped my own loneliness through my work. This has given me a sense of solidarity with others in an abstract sense that was not nearly as painful or disturbing as I would later find love and marriage to be. [13]

With her female characters, as with the Indians, she rejected the conventional stereotypes of mother, virgin, spinster, whore, etc., in favor of a wider spectrum of psychological portraits of individuals who must confront, respond to, or flee from the changing circumstances of their lives. These women, like the Indians, live in an atmosphere of conflict and frustration in which their motivating force is a desire to come to terms with themselves and the society of which they are a part, and to establish for themselves a degree of dignity and authenticity.

Conflict and Counterpoint

Castellanos's characters live in a world of multiple conflicts that serves as the motivating force of their actions. Although there are conflicts from without and from within affecting their lives, the dominant one is the clash of the Indian and the Ladino cultures. The Ladinos find their entire system of values—civic, moral, and religious—subordinated to an overriding mixture of fear and hatred of the Indians. In the case of the latter, it is not just their entirely different way of life and their relationship to nature and the supernatural that constitutes their most serious problem. Rather it is the constant humiliation and dehumanization that they suffer at the hands of the Ladinos:

Each group has its own attitude that corresponds to its particular circumstances. In the Indian a centuries-long servitude has diminished, if not annihilated, any sense of personal dignity. Humiliation had become such a habit, and misfortune has wounded them so deeply, that they have come to despise even themselves, thus becoming not just victims, but also their victimizers' willing accomplices. As for the Ladino, his sense of superiority has reached the most monstrous proportions. He lives it daily, like an immutable, biological fact of nature, and he justifies it with religious, intellectual, and historical rationalizations. [14]

Castellanos, applying Simone Weil's "two-edged sword" philosophy, makes the point that this conflict—"this relationship between Indian and Ladino that totally ignores any thought of justice"—degrades not only the victimized Indian but the victimizing Ladino as well ("Prólogo," 5). He has little opportunity to benefit from his exploitation of the Indian, for he is beset by problems that his actions have brought about and by the effect his debasing actions and attitudes have had on his own personality. The Indian, for his part, suffers not only at the hands of his *caxlán* neighbor but is also a victim of his own cosmology.[15] The author, though sympathetic to the Indian, does not gloss over the negative effects of his primitive beliefs and superstitions, his ceremonial alcoholism, or of the interpersonal conflicts that are as much a part of the Indian community as they are of the Ladino world.

In addition to the interracial conflict, there is also conflict within each racial group, primarily within families, between individuals of differing ideologies, and, most often, between male and female characters. The same exploitation that the dominating Ladino uses to degrade the Indian and himself is seen again in many of the interpersonal relationships within the two communities. The weaker members of both societies, particularly the women, have come to accept the superiority and the domination of the stronger members and thus become their exploiters' willing accomplices. Their humiliation, like the Indians', has become an accepted part of their daily existence and results in the same diminished or destroyed sense of personal worth that is evident in the lives of the Indian characters.

The many levels of conflict that affect Castellanos's characters are highlighted by their other unifying element: the use of significant contrast or counterpoint. There are contrasts of myth and reality, of myth and history, of appearance and reality, of hope and failure, of present and remembered past, of interior and exterior worlds, of dual views of time and space, of narrative point of view, of theme and of tone. Whether the conflicts are Indian/Ladino, male/female, upper class/lower class, idealist/realist, strong/weak, old/young, master/servant, or parent/child, the characters represent different world views that come into sharper focus when seen in contrast with one another. Character portrayal itself assumes a contrapuntal style, as one serves as foil to the other or is seen through the eyes of another, or when counterpart characters fulfill parallel roles within their respective communities.

The counterpoint roles of dominator/dominated, exploiter/exploited, victimizer/victim, provide the common denominator that runs throughout the works, whether occurring between the two racial groups that live in Chiapas or in the conflictive interpersonal relationships that exist within each group. In all cases, it is the counterpoint that plays the conflicting parts against one another and, in so doing, brings each into clearer perspective.

In Search of "El Otro"

Because of the autobiographical nature of Rosario Castellanos's writing and the interesting evolution of her works in various genres, some knowledge of her life and total literary output can provide valuable insight into the understanding of the interrelationship of her personal experiences and her artistic production. Conflict and counterpoint are seen in her personal life as clearly as in her works, and her writings in poetry, drama, and the essay serve as valuable complements to her novels and stories, shedding new light on their meaning and purpose.

Her desire was to portray life as she saw it, not according to any creed, but from the realities of her life. Her characters, besides being recreations of people she knew, also represented a vital part of her own inner self:

If I were not a writer, I would like to have been the protagonist of a novel. Actually, that is how I first came to discover my literary calling. I yearned for a kind of existence that was clear, direct, perfect, unalterable, and eternal. The setting in which I would like to have moved was the pages of a book. Since these dreams were impossible, I was left with no choice but to fill the pages of books myself and to invent and develop characters, giving them a history and a destiny. And, as it turned out, while I was creating them, I was creating myself as well. [16]

This need to create a meaningful existence echoes a similar expression made years before in her verses. Rosario had come to know the reality of rejection and personal pain at an early age. She also learned to rechannel her anguish into the words of her poetry. She confirmed that writing provided an escape from loneliness and fulfilled her need for artistic expression:

> With the wisdom of one who practices
> his profession with skill,
> the reporter asks: "Why do you write?"
>
> But, sir, it's quite obvious. Because someone
> (when I was little)
> said that people like me don't exist.
> Because their bodies don't project a shadow,
> because they don't make a weight on the scales,
> because their names are among those that are easily forgotten.
> And then. . . . But no, it's not that simple.
>
> I write because one day when I was an adolescent,
> I looked into a mirror and no one was there.
> Can you believe it? Complete nothingness.
> And then, beside me "others"
> assumed great importance. [17]

"I can always write," she told her friend Elena Poniatowska, "even when things are not going well, when I am depressed, I sit down at my desk, I become completely absorbed, and I forget everything bad." [18]

Writing became her method of working her way through the many conflicts of her life. It served as a means of poetic unburdening and gave her a sense of dignity and self-worth. Later it became the vehicle for reliving her childhood experiences and for expressing her sense of solidarity with the human community. "I came to poetry after convincing myself that I could not survive by any other means. And in those years what interested me most was survival. Poetic words are the only means of achieving anything lasting in this world." [19]

Hers was a committed art, a life devoted to serving others. She was a person who, in spite of the contradictions and conflicts of her own existence, gave freely of herself to others, was genuinely concerned for the well-being of her fellowman, and was ever reaching out to touch the lives of other people. As Elena Poniatowska expressed it: "I always had the impression that Rosario went about among people with a flower in her hand looking for someone to give it to." [20] This sense of solidarity with humanity finds eloquent expression in one of her earliest poems, "El otro" (Someone Else):

> Why speak the names of gods, stars,
> foam on an invisible ocean,

pollen from the remotest gardens?
If life causes us pain, if each day dawns
tearing at our innermost being, if each night falls
convulsed and afflicted.
If we feel pain for someone, for some man
we do not know, but who is
present at every hour and is the victim
and the enemy and love and all
that we lack to be whole.
Never say that the darkness is yours alone,
don't swallow your happiness in a single gulp.
Look around you: there's someone else, there's always someone else. . . .

(*Poesía*, 109)

Again in the poem "Poesía no eres tú" (Poetry Isn't You), often called her *ars poetica*, she makes a similar statement. Rather than Gustavo Adolfo Bécquer's romantic ideal, as stated in his "Poesía eres tú" (Poetry Is You), communication with others is the primary motive for Rosario's poetic expression:

Someone else: mediator, judge, balance
between opposites, witness,
knot with which one ties up what had been broken.

Someone else, muteness that seeks a voice
from one who has a voice
and claims the ear of one who listens.

Someone else. With someone else
humanity, dialogue, and poetry begin.

(*Poesía*, 301–2)

In solitude she sought companionship, a fellow human being, a "someone else" with whom to share her thoughts and dreams, a "profound dialogue that annuls the 'I' and the 'you' to create a 'we,' a new 'I' that breaks this devastating loneliness."[21] But no one was there, and as a result she began to express her thoughts and innermost feelings in writing, first in a faithfully kept diary (that would later provide source material for her literary works), then in occasional poems: "In order to exorcise the ghosts that surrounded me I had nothing but words . . . !"[22] She further tells us that:

When I began to write, I felt that all around me was confusion, and that poetry was my attempt to clarify things, to put them in order, to understand them.

When I was ten I published my first poem. Immediately I felt "published." I knew that I would be a writer forever. Of course I later had doubts. In an environment like that of Chiapas it is quite unnatural for a woman to be a writer. "Why am I doing this?" I would ask myself. "It has nothing to do with real life. It's a kind of abnormal excretion."[23]

Even in these early poems she began to express feelings that were to become a lingering part of her philosophy of life and artistic purpose:

I discovered at a very early age that heart and passion, love and pain were inseparable terms, since they rhyme nicely in Spanish, and that led me not only to a tainted theme and form but also to a concept of life and the world from which I still suffer consequences [El uso, 15–16]. I would think about things, imagine things. I imagined that I was dead. Then to give greater substance to my thoughts I began to write them down. Soon, I realized that the act of writing had somehow diminished my anguish and my sensation of solitude and non-existence.[24]

Just as her writing provided a much needed outlet for her pent-up feelings of emptiness, so the world of books provided an escape from loneliness. She confessed that "I felt foolish, unattractive, that no one loved me. My parents didn't notice because I read and read without revealing anything. Today I've had to recover a lot of ground that I lost in those days."[25]

Her only companions, besides those found in books, were Indians—her *nana;* her *cargadora,* or Indian playmate; and the others that attended the family.[26] From them, and at an impressionable age, she came to understand the Indian point of view and way of life which she was to depict so naturally in her novels and stories. In all the time she spent alone, isolated in closed-off rooms, her impressions were distilled, and from their essence her stories were born.[27]

A Feminist Perspective

Castellanos continued to search for her niche, for a perfection of her artistic expression, convinced that:

> There must be another way. . . .
> Another way to be human and free.
> Another way to be.
>
> (*Poesía,* 316)

In her quest for authenticity of purpose, she joined the ranks of other contemporary Hispanic writers—Elena Garro, Luisa Josefina Hernández, Elena

Poniatowska, Magdalena Mondragón, María Luisa Bombal, Silvina Bullrich, Josefina Vicens, Silvina Ocampo, and many others—as they sought to establish their own personal identities as women and as creative artists.

Elena Poniatowska explained how much those of the younger generation of women writers owed to Castellanos's pioneering spirit:

Rosario was . . . great . . . not only for herself but for all of us—those who would come after. She opened wide the door of feminist literature and initiated it. In a certain way it is thanks to her that those of us who attempt to write are able to do so. Before her, no one but Sor Juana—and she is a dazzling phenomenon quite apart from all the rest —truly devoted herself to her vocation. No one else really lived to write. Rosario is finally just that: a creator, a maker of books. Her books—both poetry and prose—are the diary of her life. . . . Her endeavors throughout her forty-nine years are a moral force; and she, more than any other feminine figure, makes life more worthwhile, more precious, and more meaningful for the rest of us. [28]

Castellanos's earliest influence was the Mexican nun of whom Poniatowska wrote. Sor Juana Inés de la Cruz (1648–95), an outspoken champion of woman's right to education, begged her mother to allow her to dress in men's clothing so that she might attend classes at the National University in a day when women's presence there was strictly forbidden. When her requests were denied, she satisfied her longing for an education by reading all the books in her grandfather's library. She wrote a resounding defense to those who criticized her intellectual endeavors and penned eloquent verses that berated "foolish men who unjustly criticize women / when you yourselves are the cause of the very things about which you complain." [29]

The first in a long line of Latin American women in search of "another way to be," Sor Juana was followed by other notable women poets who wrote of the feminine experience with extraordinary passion and intensity. Castellanos made frequent reference to these, her literary forebears, and remarked that "I owe Juana de Ibarbourou my incurable lack of confidence in sensual themes, to Delmira Agustini my precautions against grandiloquence, and to Alfonsina Storni the discovery of irony as an interesting perspective and the zeal for experimentation, for breaking established molds, and for accepting the unpleasant as a valid possibility." [30]

The writer who had the most profound impact on her work, however, was Latin America's first Nobel laureate, Gabriela Mistral. Traces of the Chilean's influence are evident throughout Castellanos's writings, for Mistral was also a poet of solitude, of maternity, of unrequited love, of concern for the plight of the poor, and for the special problems of women. Like Castellanos, she found solace for her own desolation through sharing the burdens and sorrows of others and, like Castellanos, was a teacher, a creative artist, a diplomat, and a woman in search of dignity and purpose.

Acknowledging her debt to Gabriela Mistral, Castellanos explained: "To find my way out of a blind alley, I found nothing more effective than placing before myself a model, an example. And then following it with the utmost fidelity. I chose Gabriela Mistral."[31]

Other influences are also apparent, many of them from outside Latin America. She felt a special kinship with the hermetical Emily Dickinson, whose poetry she translated into Spanish and whose words serve as epitaph for her tomb. She also admired Virginia Woolf and wrote an essay on her works, which she subtitled "literature as an exercise in liberty," a declaration of the freedom to be oneself.

Perhaps the strongest intellectual influence upon the work of Rosario Castellanos came from France, from the existentialist Simone de Beauvoir and from the social and religious thinker Simone Weil. Both are cited frequently by Castellanos in her essays and in her conversations. The confluence of their lives and their works lies principally in the study of human relationships, their involvement with "el otro." In this context Castellanos has been called "the Simone de Beauvoir of Mexico," as she reaffirms the notion that traditional ideologies perpetuate oppression and that the oppressed are so conditioned that they willingly consent to their oppression.[32] Her debt to the other Simone, in a similar vein, is expressed in these words to interviewer Emmanuel Carballo:

The reading of Simone Weil was of great help to me—I say Simone Weil because I don't know of any other authors who could have been more useful. She offers, within the social life, a series of constants that determine the attitude of the oppressed in the face of their oppressors, the treatment that the strong give the weak, the picture of the reactions of the subjugated, the current of evil that flows from the strong to the weak and then back to the strong once more. This kind of contagion struck me as painful and fascinating.[33]

Drawing on such divergent influences, Castellanos fused her aesthetic inclinations with a continuing concern for the individual, in particular that oppressed individual she saw in the female of the species. As early as her first attempts at poetry, her thematic insistence was on the dilemma and indignity suffered by womankind.

She expressed her own personal perspective in the form of a poetic "I," a *persona* that appears again and again, nowhere more vividly than in "Lecciones de cosas" (Lessons About Things):

They taught me all wrong,
these people who teach things:
parents, teachers, priests
all told me: you have to be good.

   .   .   .   .   .   .

I obeyed. Everybody knows that
obedience is the greatest virtue.

   .   .   .   .   .

And I sat down to wait for the medal or the sweet reward
and the smile, the prize, after all, of this world.
And I only met with scorn for my weakness,

   .   .   .   .

Until I understood. And I made of myself
a well-oiled screw with which
the machine now works satisfactorily.

(Poesía, 297–99)

Once more in first person she paints a poetic "Autorretrato" (Self-portrait), contrasting a wife's traditional role in marriage to her own frustration and disillusion:

I'm a Mrs.: a fact
difficult to accomplish in my case,
yet more useful in dealing with others
than any academic degree conferred upon me.

And so, I flaunt my trophy and repeat:
I'm a Mrs. . . .

   .   .   .

I would be happy if I knew how.
I mean, if they had taught me the proper gestures,
the small talk, the decorations.

Instead they taught me how to cry. But crying
is a broken mechanism in me;
and I don't cry at funerals
or on sublime occasions
or in the face of catastrophe.

I cry when I burn the rice or when I lose
the latest receipt for the property taxes.

(Poesía, 288–90)

Castellanos also drew other poetic portraits, memorable female images—Dido, Eve, Judith, Salomé, the Indian figures of mother, washerwoman, and fruitseller—who gave eternal testimony to woman's strength in the face of adversity. Wives, mothers, spinsters, and nursemaids appear, patiently enduring the bonds of traditional servitude, like the women in these lines from "Sobre mesa" (Around the Table):

> After the meal they linger
> around the table. And there
> the men smoke their cigarettes;
> the women go about their work,
> its origins so remote as to
> be scarcely remembered. Black coffee
> steams in cups often refilled.
>
> Someone cuts the pages of a book
> or gathers up bread crumbs with her fingers,
> and the one over there counts the months
> of her pregnancy to another who has
> finished raising her children. . . .
>
> (*Poesía,* 191)

Single women, however, those who have no place in a society based on pairs, suffer the loneliness and alienation of not belonging:

> It's shameful to be alone.
> A terrible blush burns on her cheek
> the whole day long . . .
>
> .   .   .   .   .   .
>
> At night the single woman
> lies down upon her bed of agony:
> An anguished sweat bursts forth to wet the sheets
> and the void is filled
> with imaginary dialogue and men.
>
> And the single woman waits, and waits, and waits.
>
> .   .   .   .
>
> And she smiles at the dawn alone.
>
> (*Poesía,* 175)

These same lonely females also fill the pages of Castellanos's novels and stories. Whether married or single, her female characters suffer isolation as marginal beings in a tradition-bound community where they are alienated from society and even from one another. They are seen not only as the victims of man's brutality, but of other women's as well. There are no caring relationships, not even between mothers and daughters. Children are reared by Indian *nanas*—the only relationship that reveals any feelings of tenderness—while their mothers struggle to maintain their positions in a male-dominated world.

Even in her earliest prose of Indian interest, Castellanos's most convincing characters are women—the neglected child, the Indian *nana*, the lonely spinster, the frustrated social worker—and culminate in the extraordinary characterization of Catalina, the barren Indian *ilol* of her final novel, *Oficio de tinieblas* (Tenebrae Service).

As the focus shifts, in her last two volumes of stories, from the Ladino/Indian conflict to the problems of contemporary urban life, female characters continue to dominate the fictional scene as they face their daily confrontations with a closed and stifling society that punishes anyone who dares to step beyond traditionally held modes of conduct. Women are seen as victims both of an accepted male dominance and of their own ingrained passivity. There are several variations on the theme of the self-sacrificing woman, as well as examples at the opposite extreme, who reject any degree of domesticity and challenge the status quo. Those who dare to break established patterns, however, invariably suffer the consequences of their assertive attitudes and actions.

Castellanos assigns equal responsibility for such injustice to men and to women, as both play roles that tend to perpetuate the prevailing oppression. As Simone de Beauvoir suggests, the one maintains a justification for his domineering stance, while the other, conditioned since time immemorial, meekly accepts her subordinate position, as if condoning her own oppression. The result is deception, mutual alienation, and total breakdown of communication.

While Castellanos mirrors these images with great effectiveness in her prose fiction, she found a more direct vehicle for expressing her thoughts on women's issues in her articles and essays.[34] Although she was reluctant to classify herself as a feminist, at least "not in the commonly-understood sense of the term," she was a pioneer in her wide-ranging application of feminist ideas to literary commentary.[35]

Sobre cultura femenina (On Feminine Culture) was the title of her master's thesis and has been called "the intellectual point of departure of the women's movement in recent years in Mexico."[36] Her *Juicios sumarios* (Summary Judgments), a collection in which she sustains "an informal chat with the world, with reality," presents perceptive essays on Santa Teresa, Sor Juana, Simone de Beauvoir, Virginia Woolf, Simone Weil, and others from around the world who had influenced her literary and philosophical formation. They are a manifestation of her concept of "literature as an exercise in liberation," and a further attempt at finding "another way to be."

The collection also includes a brief essay in which Castellanos discusses the three most important feminine archetypes in Mexico: the Virgin of Guadalupe, Malinche, and Sor Juana. The first is venerated even beyond the realm of religion and represents the quintessential good; the second is a sex object, dangerous, seductive, placing in jeopardy both moral and cultural values; the third is the feminist par excellence, a woman whose beauty is rivaled only by her intelligence, quick wit, and moral courage.

The volume that most overtly expresses Castellanos's thoughts on the status of women, however, is *Mujer que sabe latín . . .* (A Woman Who Knows Latin . . .). In this collection of essays, called "the first feminist book written by a Mexican woman of reknown," she addresses the unique problems of Mexican women and encourages them to achieve their full potential as persons.[37] She instructs the Mexican male that: "Nothing enslaves quite like the act of enslaving; nothing produces a greater degradation in oneself than that which one attempts to inflict upon another. And if a man grants a woman the degree of personhood that up to now has been denied her, then he himself will be enriched and his character as a person who is willing to give will become more solid" (*Mujer,* 38).

She confronts her reader with the contradictions inherent in women's situation and reveals "aspects of life's daily patterns that are ridiculous, obsolete, vulgar, and silly" (*Mujer,* 39). In one such article she points out that Mexican society in general has been as much to blame for woman's unfortunate position as "an inferior, ancillary being"[38] as has been her male counterpart:

From birth onward, a woman's education is at work, adapting her to her destiny, developing her into a morally acceptable being, that is, socially useful. And so she is robbed of her initiative to make decisions, taught to obey the mandates of an ethic that is absolutely foreign to her and which has no justification or any foundation except to serve the interests, designs, and purposes of other people. (*Mujer,* 14)

In a letter to a North American writer who had asked permission to translate the collection, she further elaborated her concern that women in Mexico, far too long willing accomplices to the prevailing injustices, need to break old patterns of submission and take charge of their lives: "In present-day Mexican society, woman will do well to emancipate herself emotionally (she has already done so economically) from the tutelage of the man in the house and to assume her full responsibility as a person."[39]

As a person, rather than as an object or marginal being, the Mexican woman can then assume, according to Castellanos, a position of dignity with complete use of her own talents and abilities. She can assume an active role in society and pursue a vocation of her own choosing—"the backbone of any human being"—rather than submit to the role that tradition has thrust upon her. In so doing she can take full advantage of "all the opportunities that will free her from being a totally helpless creature," for as Castellanos goes on to point out: "Since women in Mexico were granted their civil rights, much has been said about the equality that was achieved. Nevertheless, the most cursory analysis of the actual circumstances clearly reveals that it is an equality like that of the Indians in their relationship to the whites: legal, but not real. For women, in fact, continue to occupy a place of confinement."[40]

We can conclude, then, that Rosario Castellanos's answer for the dilemma of the Mexican woman is to be found in an enlightened attitude on the part of all segments of society and the freedom to become an active, equal participant in the community. In this way she, like the Indian, can achieve self-respect and her own identity as a person. Castellanos's struggle for women's rights thus becomes a part of a larger ideal: the search for justice and dignity for all oppressed people.

The New Mexican Woman

Castellanos stated on numerous occasions that her major purpose in writing was to "explain to myself all that which I do not understand"[41] and to raise the level of consciousness of her readers to the injustices about them so as to awaken a critical spirit that will prevent them from accepting any dogma "without first seeing whether or not it can withstand a good joke" (*Mujer,* 40). That "good joke" was finally perpetrated by Castellanos in her last work, the delightful dramatic farce *El eterno femenino* (The Eternal Feminine).

In this product of the latter phase of her creative evolution, Castellanos leaves behind the solitude and melancholy of the past and turns joyfully to a combination of humor and wit to achieve her artistic purposes. Through her poetry she freed her soul of its personal anguish as she sounded the depths of her own despair. In her prose fiction she held up a mirror to the prevailing injustices of her native land. With this comedy, she inaugurates a new vein. Moved by the same commitment to truth that characterizes her previous works, Castellanos unmasks hypocrisy, dispels myth, and challenges the status quo, as she continues to convey the dilemmas faced by women living in a man's world.

She poses the same questions as before, but she couches them in a new language and portrays them in a new light. The setting is a contemporary social scene, the characters cartoon-like images whose often-grotesque nature makes them no less endearing. They are stereotype figures from the present and the past—Juan and Lupita, Adam and Eve, Cortés and Malinche, Maximilian and Carlotta, and many more—who "strut and fret their hour upon the stage" in gleeful mockery of the world in which they live. Their common denominator is a dialogue that sparkles with both humor and pathos, leaving the audience wondering whether to laugh or to cry.

The late-blooming Castellanos wit was also enjoyed by the students in her literature classes at the Hebrew University in Jerusalem. Nahum Megged, her close friend in Israel, told of her vibrance and dynamism in the classroom:

Rosario would take a serious theme and turn it into a joke. The students didn't know when to stop laughing, and by the time they reached their homes, they realized that they had forgotten the jokes, retaining only a deep, rich subsoil into which had been sown a powerful capacity for understanding. For Rosario talked about serious and often terribly tragic things, but since she wrapped them in a cloak of humor and crystal, they were not immediately perceived as such.[42]

This same comment might also be made of Castellanos's essays and the poetry that flowed from her pen during these last years of her life. There was a new sense of humor and a lighter touch, a sense of having come to full attainment of her own poetic voice, described by Carlos Monsiváis as "humor in the face of everyday disaster."[43] Using the magical weapons of a wry tongue-in-cheek tone and colloquial language ("I now feel free to depart from the prescribed rules"[44]), she deals lightly with those subjects that had once caused her despair. Love, for example, "the great father of so much pain and the goal of the romantics,"[45] which she once called "a catastrophic element,"[46] loses its bitterness in a poem called "Consejo de Celestina" (A Matchmaker's Advice). Marriage, another subject of disillusionment for Castellanos, is divested of its tragic overtones when treated with the new realism of "Kinsey Report":

Am I married? This means
that a license was made out in someone's office
and in time it turned yellow
and there was a church ceremony
with attendants and everything. And a banquet
and an entire week in Acapulco.

No, I can't wear my wedding dress anymore.
I've put on weight with the children
and the problems. As you can see,
there are plenty of those.

> With a frequency that I can predict
> my husband makes use of his rights, or,
> as he likes to say, he pays his conjugal
> debt. Then he turns his back on me. And snores. . . .
>
> (Poesía, 317)

Motherhood, the traditional Mexican woman's raison d'être, loses some of its aura when pregnancy is described as a realistic series of physiological aggravations in "Se habla de Gabriel" (Speaking of Gabriel):

> Ugly, sick, bored,
> I felt it grow at my expense,
> steal its color from my blood, add
> weight and clandestine volume
> to my way of being upon the earth.
>
> .   .   .   .
>
> And through the wound by which it departed
> through that hemorrhage of its turning loose
> also departed the last vestage of my solitude,
> of my lonely self gazing out from behind a glass.
>
> (Poesía, 291)

In the last lines of this poem, Castellanos couches the revealing statement that the birth of her son Gabriel, referred to elsewhere as "my art of love,"[47] brought to an end the solitude that for so long had haunted her life.[48] Perhaps it is this personal rebirth that freed her from her melancholy and released her spirit so that it was able to seek new and more optimistic forms of expression. "One must laugh, then," she tells us, "since laughter, as we know, is the first manifestation of freedom" (*Mujer*, 207).

Rosario Castellanos had by now come to understand the dignity of her own person, and the result was a new freedom to be herself, as a writer and as a woman: "Woman must assume her role as a person, she must repect herself, she must love herself, because one cannot give to another that which one does not grant oneself."[49]

With this new understanding of herself, she came to view even the things she held most sacred with the more lighthearted attitude that was evident in her last poems. The following passage, a condensed version of a longer article, illustrates the extent to which she had come to look with new and happier perspective on the painful aspects of her life. It also serves as a summary of the major events in her life, related this time with humor, and deals with the theme that haunted her from childhood, solitude:

Let us recapitulate. First, an only child, not allowed to attend school regularly. . . . Abandoned during my adolescence to the resources of my imagination. . . . I remained single until the age of 32, during which time I suffered periods of extreme isolation, confined in a tuberculosis sanitorium, serving in an institute for Indians. . . . Add to this the fact that I am very shy and that, unless I was forced to do so, I never attended parties for fear of having to mix and mingle with other people. . . . What is your diagnosis? The same as mine: This woman is an oyster!

But remember that the term "solitude" cannot be fully understood unless one compares it to its opposite: "companionship." And that is where I put my cat out to play. In order to feel "accompanied" I almost never felt the need of the physical presence of another when I was a child. I talked to myself, because I am a Gemini. While still very young I had already begun to write verses. And what was the result of my first love interest? The writing of an intimate diary . . . , a chronicle which later served me well as a source of stories, novels, and poems.

With time my resources have multiplied—reading . . . , listening to the radio . . . , and, of course, this article, which you must admit, is much like a pleasant chat.

Nevertheless, there comes a time when I have to admit that I am a totally helpless creature, and my eyes fill with tears thinking about the fact that I am orphaned and divorced and that, had they lived, my children would be older than Gabriel and the little girl would be going to dances and having boyfriends and would think that I am a monster who doesn't understand her and who is rearing her all wrong. . . .

That terrible moment when I come to the full realization of my solitude and the unbearable anathema with which I am cursed, is the moment when I have finished putting on my makeup and getting dressed, and find that there is no one around to zip up my zipper. There are no arms that can properly execute this important operation. If someone else is in the house, fine. But in a hotel, is one to call upon the chamber maid—who often turns out to be a chamber man—to bear witness to our humiliation? Never. So one twists and turns and goes one's way, feeling a bit like a chrysalid that wonders if it will ever escape its cocoon because it anticipates a return to that empty room where there is no one to unzip zippers and where one dares not ask this favor of one's *chevalier servant* for fear he might take it as an overture of the worst possible taste, which would alter the order of cause and effect and everything else. . . .

Tel Aviv, 19 June 1973
(*El uso*, 293–96)

The article from which this passage is taken, with the good-humored style of her last years, attests to the fact that Rosario Castellanos had at last found satisfactory resolution of the emotional conflicts of her younger days, a new serenity and a personal peace from which she was able to reach out to others, and in her own way, "through the use of the word." Now she can smile at those very things that had most seriously troubled her and could affirm with Julio Cortázar that indeed "laughter has always dug more tunnels than tears."[50]

This happy phase of her life, as well as her promising career, was cut short, however, when an electrical accident in her Tel Aviv residence took her life on 7 August 1974.[51] Her body was returned to her homeland and, as it lay in state in the Palace of Fine Arts in Mexico City, a group of Chamula Indians stood guard nearby. She was accorded all the honors of a state funeral and was buried in the Rotunda of Illustrious Men, the first and only woman writer to be so honored.

There were many tributes paid her at the time of her death and many laudatory commentaries on the nature of her life and works. But the words that best express the essence of the rich legacy she left behind are found in a statement of her own: "Love is recognizing that others exist. That they are free and have a right to happiness. Love is neither possessing nor being possessed, but rather communicating with one another."[52]

Poetry

Let poetry be like a key
that opens a thousand doors.
        —Vicente Huidobro, "Ars poetica"

We only came here to know
one another, we are upon this
earth but for a little while.
        —anonymous Nahuatl poem

. . . I had to grow up fast
(before terror devoured me),
get out on my own, keep a firm hand
on things and take hold of life.
        —Rosario Castellanos,
            "Monólogo de la extranjera"

Reproach hath broken my heart, and I am full of heaviness; and I
looked for some to take pity, but there was none; and for comforters,
but I found none.
        —Psalms 69:20

Poetry was the earliest and most consistently cultivated genre of Rosario Caste-llanos's multifaceted literary production. Moreover, it may well be the clearest key to understanding her creative evolution, while providing intimate insight into the interpretation of all her works.

Her rich poetic legacy consists of the twelve titles that she herself compiled as *Poesía no eres tú* (Poetry Isn't You) in 1972, along with a few isolated poems and the uncollected poetry of her Tel Aviv period (1971–74). Inspired principally by the works of Sor Juana, Gabriela Mistral, Jorge Guillén, José Gorostiza, and the Bible, Rosario Castellanos's poetry moves from the declama-tory, rhetorical style of her early collections to the lighter, more colloquial— often tongue-in-cheek—tone found in her later verse. The developing counter-point of abstract/concrete, image/idea, lyric/narrative is evident throughout and reflects similar contrasts seen in her prose. Her initial search for meaning and purpose in her own life gives way to a heightened interest in the world about her and a deep commitment to fellowship and communion with other human beings.

Her first book of poems, *Trayectoria del polvo* (Trajectory of Dust; 1948), which she described as "a sort of summary of my understanding of life, my-self, and others," [1] was written in a week's time after a reading of Mexican poet José Gorostiza's *Muerte sin fin* (Death Without End). It was an extensive work that gave poetic utterance to her grief at the death of both her parents within one month in 1948, a period of psychoanalysis, and a religious crisis. [2] She explained, "I assumed that the best way to express myself was in a long poem of great unburdening. . . ." [3]

Dedicating herself exclusively to her writing, she published in that same year another volume, *Apuntes para una declaración de fe* (Notes for a Declaration of Faith; 1948), in which she wrote that "the world howls as sterile as a mush-room." [4] "I added, for an original touch, the deliberate use of commonplaces and prosaisms in order to paint a dark picture of the contemporary world." [5]

After these two works, she began to move away from abstraction and poems of extended length. "I no longer wanted to write intellectual poems," she wrote. "My desire was to write poems that were, if not emotional, at least filled with images of concrete things." [6] The next volume, *De la vigilia esteril* (Of the Sterile Vigil; 1950) was a step in that direction: "The poems were less vague, more modest with respect to theme (I was by then beginning to discover my individuality and the validity with which poetry expresses one's varying moods) and more concise with regard to form" (*Juicios*, 431).

Poetry had by now become her life. She traveled to Spain, where she studied stylistics under the tutelage of Nobel laureate Vicente Aleixandre, but through her European experience she realized that the country she had come to know best was the one she had left behind:

The fact of having been in Spain gave us—by contrast—a keener awareness of Mexico. In our country we were always so submerged in everyday life that we never appreciated our own distinctiveness. Comparing the customs of the two countries, we came to discover many characteristics of our own and many ways of being, of understanding, and, in short, of living.[7]

When she returned to Mexico in 1951, it was with a fresh appreciation for her country's cultural uniqueness. She went almost directly to Chiapas to work for the Institute of Arts and Sciences in Tuxtla Gutiérrez, convinced that an educated person should share her knowledge with those who are less fortunate. Stirred by this new consciousness and her increasing sense of solidarity with her Chiapanecan heritage, she wrote her next collection of poems, *El rescate del mundo* (Rescue of the World; 1952). The "rescued world" herein described is the familiar scene of her childhood, rediscovered and reclaimed as she worked there among its Indians. The poems represent a further move away from the abstraction of her earlier verses and achieve a naturalness not seen before. "I tried to capture an object like a spark from a fire," she explained, "two or three images on the same theme."[8]

Her next book, *Poemas 1953–1955* (Poems 1953–1955; 1957), provided her even greater satisfaction: "The various influences I was attempting to acknowledge were reconciled and combined harmoniously for the first time, and I was able to integrate and transmit a coherent concept of things and establish a true relationship between them and myself" (*Juicios*, 432). "Among the objects that surrounded me," she continued, "I tried to find those that were most significant, most essential, those that allowed me to integrate my own vision of the world"—a world where it was possible to be "bound to things from an emotional point of view . . . treating them as objects of aesthetic contemplation."[9]

With the publication of her subsequent volumes, *Al pie de la letra* (Word for Word; 1959), *Lívida luz* (Livid Light; 1960), and *Materia memorable* (Memorable Matter; 1969), she at last began to recognize her own poetic voice. Ironic and nostalgic, conversational and compassionate, the language of her verse grew more flexible and more precise: "I could see . . . three cardinal points starting to emerge: humor, solemn meditation, and contact with my physical and historical roots. And all bathed in the 'Livid Light' of death, which makes all matter memorable." [10]

Castellanos's poetry is indeed all "memorable matter." Whether the simplest lyric or the most complex image, it brings us themes of the deepest human concern: loneliness, love, death, affirmation, and hope. From the "rescued world" of Chiapas to the final engagement with humankind, the poems reveal the consummate skill of a creative artist who longed to draw in her reader to share her poetic world. "Fellowman," she wrote, "wherever you are, wherever you live, there shall we all remain" (Poesía, 185).

I have chosen to make this section bilingual in the sincere hope that readers will benefit from seeing the original Spanish alongside the English rendition. Translation of poetry is, at best, only an attempt to transcend the barrier of language and style. As Stanley Burnshaw explains in his introduction to the book *The Poem Itself*: "The instant [the reader] departs from the words of the original, he departs from *its* poetry. For the words are the poem. An English translation is always a different thing: it is always an *English* poem."

And so, I urge you to refer to the original often, and to read it aloud, even if you understand little, if any, of what is written there. For the poem is also the sound, the rhythm, the meter, and that is often lost in the translation.

It has been said—obviously by a man—that translated poetry is rather like a woman: if she's beautiful, she's not faithful, and if she's faithful, she's not beautiful. In these translations of Rosario Castellanos's poems, I have attempted to be, above all, faithful to the original—to the tone as well as to the thought and the words themselves. The beauty I leave to the eye of the beholder.

I have chosen the following selections in an endeavor to show the many facets of Castellanos's poetry, as well as the remarkable variety of its content and style. If these translations help to awaken an interest in her poetry, if they contribute in any way to a broader appreciation of her work, then I shall feel gratified indeed.

Apuntes para una declaración de fe

El mundo gime estéril como un hongo.
Es la hoja caduca y sin viento en otoño,
la uva pisoteada en el lagar del tiempo
pródiga en zumos agrios y letales.
Es esta rueda isócrona fija entre cuatro cirios,
esta nube exprimida y paralítica
y esta sangre blancuzca en un tubo de ensayo.

La soledad trazó su paisaje de escombros.
La desnudez hostil es su cifra ante el hombre.

Sin embargo, recuerdo . . .

En un día de amor yo bajé hasta la tierra:
vibraba como un pájaro crucificado en vuelo
y olía a hierba húmeda, a cabellera suelta,
a cuerpo traspasado de sol al mediodía.
Era como un durazno o como una mejilla
y encerraba la dicha
como los labios encierran un beso.

Ese día de amor yo fui como la tierra:
sus jugos me sitiaban tumultuosos y dulces
y la raíz bebía con mis poros el aire
y un rumor galopaba desde siempre
para encontrar los cauces de mi oreja.
Al través de mi piel corrían las edades:
se hacía la luz, se desgarraba el cielo
y se extasiaba—eterno—frente al mar.
El mundo era la forma perpetua de asombro
renovada en el ir y venir de la ola,
consubstancial al giro de la espuma
y el silencio, una simple condición de las cosas. . . .

[Fragment; from *Apuntes para una declaración de fe*, 1948, in *Poesía no eres tú*, 1972]

Notes for a Declaration of Faith

The world groans, sterile as a mushroom.
It is the dying, windless leaf in autumn,
the grape crushed in the winepress of time
rich in bitter, lethal juices.
It is this isochronous wheel fixed between four candles,
this cloud, pressed and paralytic
and this whitish blood of a test tube.

Solitude traced its landscape of refuse.
Hostile barrenness is its cryptic code before mankind.

Nevertheless, I remember . . .

One day of love I descended to the earth:
it moved like a bird crucified in flight
and smelled of damp herbs, of loosened hair,
of a body transfixed by the noonday sun.
It was like a peach or like a cheek
and it encircled joy
as lips encircle a kiss.

That day of love I was like the earth:
its sweet, tumultuous juices besieged me
and the root drank in air through my pores
and a murmur raced from forever
to seek the deepest recesses of my ear.
Through my skin the ages ran:
light was made, the sky was rent
and found eternal ecstasy near the sea.
The world was the perpetual shape of awe
renewed in the ebb and flow of the waves,
at one with the whirling of the foam
and silence, a simple condition of all things. . . .

Muro de lamentaciones

II

Detrás de mí tan sólo las memorias borradas.
Mis muertos ni trascienden de sus tumbas
y por primera vez estoy mirando el mundo.

Soy hija de mí misma.
De mi sueño nací. Mi sueño me sostiene.

No busquéis en mis filtros más que mi propia sangre
ni remontéis los ríos para alcanzar mi origen.

En mi genealogía no hay más que una palabra:
Soledad.

V

Entre las cosas busco Tu huella y no la encuentro.
Lo que mi oído toca se convierte en silencio,
la orilla en que me tiendo se deshace.

¿Dónde estás? ¿Por qué apartas tu rostro de mi rostro?
¿Eres la puerta enorme que esconde la locura,
el muro que devuelve lamento por lamento?

Esperanza,
¿eres sólo una lápida?

[Fragment; from *De la vigilia estéril*, 1950, in *Poesía no eres tú*, 1972]

Wailing Wall

II

Behind me only forgotten memories.
My dead refuse to transcend their tombs
and for the first time I am seeing the world.

I am my own child.
I was born from my dream. My dream sustains me.

Seek nothing in my veins but my own blood
nor search the rivers for my origins.

In my genealogy there is only one word:
Solitude.

V

I seek Your footprints everywhere but I find them not.
All that falls upon my ears turns to silence,
the shores on which I lie become but shifting sands.

Where are you? Why do you turn your face from me?
Are you the massive door where madness hides,
the wall that returns weeping for wailing?

Hope,
are you no more than stone?

Baño ritual en el Grijalva

A la orilla del río clamoroso,
oscuros y desnudos como lirios nocturnos,
los jóvenes indígenas caminan.
Ante su piel elástica los soles retroceden
y la arena persigue sus plantas por besarlas.
Como mazorcas blancas
sonrisas cautelosas se desgranan.
Una secreta afinidad enlaza
su perfil modelado por el viento
con el perfil del polvo que viola las praderas,
pues la vehemencia late en su reposo
como una brasa oculta entre cenizas.
Invaden los imperios fluviales, impasibles,
con una calma mineral de estatua.
Tocan las algas y se vuelven verdes.
Abandonan la cárcel de sus cuerpos
ciegamente cautivos de una raza
y brevemente libres, participan
del ágil, silencioso retozo de los peces.
Después, como el lagarto, sabio de la pereza,
se extienden en la playa.
De las aguas sin treguas se retiran
sus miradas anfibias ya saciadas.

[Written at Comitán, Chiapas, on 5 November 1948. Previously unpublished. A gift from
Rosario to her friend Oscar Bonifaz on returning to Comitán from a vacation on her ranch.]

Ritual Bath in the Grijalva

On the shore of the clamorous river,
dark and naked like nocturnal lilies,
the Indian children stroll.
In the presence of their elastic skin the sunbeams fade
and the sand sprinkles kisses on their toes.
Like ears of white corn
shy smiles burst forth.
A secret affinity joins
their profile, sculptured by the wind,
to the contour of the dust that violates the meadows,
while yearning throbs in their repose
like a hidden coal among the ashes.
They invade the fluvial empire, impassively,
with the mineral calm of statues.
They touch the algae and become green.
They abandon the prison of their bodies
blindly captive by their race
and briefly free, join
the agile, silent frolic of the fishes.
Afterwards, like a lizard wise in its sloth,
they stretch out upon the sand.
From the relentless waters they retire
their now-satiated amphibious gaze.

Lavanderas del Grijalva

Pañuelo del adiós,
camisa de la boda,
en el río, entre peces
jugando con las olas.

Como un recién nacido
bautizado, esta ropa
ostenta su blancura
total y milagrosa.

Mujeres de la espuma
y el ademán que limpia,
halladme un río hermoso
para lavar mis días.

[From *El rescate del mundo,* 1952, in *Poesía no eres tú,* 1972]

Washerwomen on the Grijalva

A handkerchief for farewells,
a wedding chemise,
in the river, among the fishes
playing in the waves.

Like a newborn child
being baptized, these bits of cloth
display their infinite
miraculous whiteness.

Women of the foam
and of gesturings that cleanse,
find me a beautiful river
to wash my days.

La oración del indio

El indio sube al templo tambaleándose,
ebrio de sus sollozos como de un alcohol fuerte.
Se para frente a Dios a exprimir su miseria
y grita con un grito de animal acosado
y golpea entre sus puños su cabeza.

El borbotón de sangre que sale por su boca
deja su cuerpo quieto.

Se tiende, se abandona, duerme en el mismo suelo
con la juncia y respira
el aire de la cera y del incienso.

Repose largamente
tu inocencia de manos que no crucificaron.
Repose tu confianza
reclinada en el brazo del Amor
como un pequeño pueblo en una cordillera.

[From *El rescate del mundo*, 1952, in *Poesía no eres tú*, 1972]

The Indian's Prayer

The Indian stumbles toward the temple,
as drunk from weeping as from strong drink.
He stops before God to pour forth his misery
and wails with the cry of a hunted animal
and beats his head with his fists.

The stream of blood that flows from his mouth
leaves his body silent.

Stretched out with abandon he sleeps
on the floor strewn with reeds and breathes
the air filled with candlewax and incense.

May your hands innocent of the crucifixion
find endless rest.
May your faith find serene repose
in the arms of Love
like a humble village on a hillside.

Madre india

Camina siempre con su carga a cuestas: el hijo y, además, mercancía pobre.

Con fatiga, traspone los cerros que la confinan y baja a la ciudad que le es hostil.

Una vez consumada la venta de lo que ofrece (y con la venta el engaño y el despojo), la madre india quiere descansar. De las calles la expulsan la insolencia de los transeúntes y la profusión y la prisa de los vehículos. Busca entonces el cobijo de los árboles, viejos conocidos suyos, en el parque. Allí está, silenciosa. Pues no habla más que con sus dioses en el templo. Habla, llorando, su oración de queja humilde, ruego doloroso y sumisiones extremas.

Al regresar la madre india a su paraje, puede vérsele pastoreando el rebaño, tejiendo las telas ásperas que defenderán a la familia del frío, preparando los escasos alimentos.

En los instantes de reposo, tiene al niño sobre su regazo. Se inclina a él con una solicitud tanto más ansiosa cuanto que es inútil. Lo contempla con unos ojos en los que el amor se funde con la culpa. La sombría profundidad de su mirada tiene un nombre: desesperanza.

Porque lo que la madre india sabe es que el horizonte de mañana será el mismo que el de hoy: miseria, ignorancia, humillaciones. Sus manos (manos a las que la maternidad debería haber llenado de dádivas), están vacías. No podrán nunca sofocar bien el grito del hambre; no verterán bálsamos sobre las llagas que abra, en las espaldas de su hijo, el fardo que ha de doblegárselas. No borrará el ceño de la dignidad ofendida.

He aquí, pues, un par de manos vacías. Manos de mendigo, manos de víctima, persiguen nuestra conciencia con la obsesiva tenacidad de los remordimientos. No, no vale aturdirse. Porque si alguien ha arrebatado a esas manos su riqueza, somos nosotros. ¿Y quién más que nosotros puede restituir de nuevo y colmar?

Indian Mother

She always walks with a load on her shoulders: her baby and, then, her simple wares.

Wearily she crosses the mountains that imprison her and descends to the hostile city below.

Once her goods are sold (or pilfered or despoiled), the Indian mother seeks rest. From the streets she is expelled by the insolence of passersby and the profusion and speed of vehicles. She takes refuge instead in the trees—her ancient, trusted friends—in the park. There she remains, in silence. She speaks only with her gods in the church. Weeping, she utters her prayer of humble complaint, her sorrowful imploring and utmost submission.

When the Indian mother returns to her village, she can be seen shepherding her flock, weaving the coarse cloth that will protect her family from the cold, preparing their meager repast.

In her brief moments of repose, she holds her baby on her lap. She hovers over him with a solicitude as anxious as it is useless. She contemplates him with eyes filled with love and guilt. The shadowy depth of her gaze has a name: despair.

For the Indian mother knows that tomorrow's horizons will be the same as today's: misery, ignorance, humiliation. Her hands (hands that motherhood should have filled with gifts), are empty. They will never be fully able to stifle her child's hungry cries, nor pour oil on wounds made by the burdens he must bear. The sorrow of dignity offended will not be forgotten.

Behold, then, a pair of empty hands. Beggar's hands, victim's hands, stalk our consciences with the obsessive tenacity of remorse. No, there is no room for bewilderment. For if anyone has taken from these hands what is rightly theirs, it is we. And who, besides us, can make restitution and fill them once more?

Oh, que el sueño desampare nuestras sienes; que la amistad nos punce como una ortiga y que la canción se pudra en nuestra boca, mientras las manos de esta mujer, de esta madre india, no puedan entregar a su hijo el pan, la luz y la justicia.

[Prose poem seen in print only once, in the newspaper *El Sol de Chiapas*'s cultural supplement, published by friends to commemorate the first anniversary of Castellanos's death.]

Oh, may sleep elude our brows, may friendship pierce our hearts like thorns, and may songs offend our mouths, as long as the hands of this woman, this Indian mother, remain unable to give her child bread, light, and justice.

Una palmera

Señora de los vientos,
garza de la llanura,
cuando te meces canta
tu cintura.

Gesto de la oración
o preludio del vuelo,
en tu copa se vierten uno a uno
los cielos.

Desde el país oscuro de los hombres
he venido, a mirarte, de rodillas.
Alta, desnuda, única.
Poesía.

[From *El rescate del mundo,* 1952, in *Poesía no eres tú,* 1972]

A Palm Tree

Lady of the winds,
heron of the plains,
when you sway
your being sings.

Gesture of prayer
or prelude to flight,
through your branches
the heavens flow.

From the dark land of men
I have come, on my knees, to behold you.
Tall, naked, singular.
Poetry.

Misterios gozosos

6

A veces, tan ligera
como un pez en el agua,
me muevo entre las cosas
feliz y alucinada.

Feliz de ser quien soy,
sólo una gran mirada:
ojos de par en par
y manos despojadas.

Seno de Dios, asombro
lejos de las palabras.

Patria mía perdida,
recobrada.

[Fragment; from *Poemas,* 1957, in *Poesía no eres tú,* 1972]

Joyful Mysteries

6

At times, as spritely
as a fish in water,
I go about among things
joyful and deluded.

Happy to be who I am,
only a sweeping glance:
eyes wide open
and empty hands.

Bosom of God, awe
that defies words.

My lost homeland,
regained.

La velada del sapo

Sentadito en la sombra
—solemne con tu bocio exoftálmico; cruel
(en apariencia, al menos, debido a la hinchazón
de los párpados); frío,
frío de repulsiva sangre fría.

Sentadito en la sombra miras arder la lámpara.

En torno de la luz hablamos y quizá
uno dice tu nombre.

(Es septiembre. Ha llovido.)

Como por el resorte de la sorpresa, saltas
y aquí estás ya, en medio de la conversación,
en el centro del grito.

¡Con qué miedo sentimos palpitar
el corazón desnudo
de la noche en el campo!

[From *Al pie de la letra,* 1959, in *Poesía no eres tú,* 1972]

The Frog's Soirée

Sitting there in the shadow
—solemn with your exophthalmic bulge; cruel
(in appearance, at least, due to your
protruding eyes); cold,
cold with your repulsive cold blood.

Sitting there in the shadow you watch the flickering lamp.

Around the light we talk and perhaps
someone speaks your name.

(It is September. It has rained.)

As if springing from surprise, you jump
and here you are now, in the midst of the conversation,
in the center of the shouting.

How fearfully we feel the beat
of the naked heart
of the night in the country!

Revelación

Lo supe de repente:
hay otro.
Y desde entonces duermo sólo a medias
y ya casi no como.

No es posible vivir
con este rostro
que es el mío verdadero
y que aún no conozco.

[From *Lívida luz*, 1960, in *Poesía no eres tú*, 1972]

Revelation

All of a sudden it came to me:
there is someone else.
And since that time I hardly sleep
and scarcely eat.

It isn't possible to live
with this countenance
that is really mine
and that I do not yet know.

Nacimiento

Estuvo aquí. Ninguno (y él menos que ninguno)
supo quién era, cómo, por qué, adónde.

Decía las palabras que los otros entienden
—las suyas no llegó a escucharlas nunca—;
se escondía en el lugar en que los otros buscan,
en su casa, en su cuerpo, en sus edades,
y sin embargo ausente siempre y mudo.

Como todos fue dueño de su vida
una hora o más y luego abrió las manos.

Entonces preguntaron: ¿era hermoso?
Ya nadie recordaba aquella superficie
que la luz disputó por alumbrar
y le fue arrebatada tantas veces.

Le inventaron acciones, intenciones. Y tuvo
una historia, un destino, un epitafio.

Y fue, por fin, un hombre.

[From *Lívida luz,* 1960, in *Poesía no eres tú,* 1972]

Birth

He was here. No one (and he less than anyone)
knew who he was, how, why, or where.

He spoke the words that others understand
—his own he never heard—;
he hid himself in the place where others look,
in his house, in his body, in his ages,
still ever absent and silent.

Like everyone else he was the master of his life
an hour or more and then he opened his hands.

Then they asked: was he beautiful?
Now no one remembered that countenance
that struggled with light to illuminate
and was beaten back so often.

They invented actions, intentions. And he had
a history, a destiny, an epitaph.

And he was, at last, a man.

Lívida luz

No puedo hablar sino de lo que sé.

Como Tomás tengo la mano hundida
en una llaga. Y duele en el otro y en mí.

¡Ah, qué sudor helado de agonía!
¡Qué convulsión de asco!

No, no quiero consuelo, ni olvido, ni esperanza.

Quiero valor para permanecer,
para no traicionar lo nuestro: el día
presente y esta luz con que se mira entero.

[From *Lívida luz,* 1960, in *Poesía no eres tú,* 1972]

Livid Light

I can only talk about what I know.

Like Thomas, I have my hand thrust in a wound.
And it gives pain to another and to me.

Oh, what icy, anguished drops of sweat!
What nauseating convulsion!

No, I care not for consolation, oblivion, or hope.

I long for courage to endure,
to betray not that which is ours: this day
and this light with which one sees all things.

Presencia

Algún día lo sabré. Este cuerpo que ha sido
mi albergue, mi prisión, mi hospital, es mi tumba.

Esto que uní alrededor de un ansia,
de un dolor, de un recuerdo,
desertará buscando el agua, la hoja,
la espora original y aun lo inerte y la piedra.

Este nudo que fui (inextricable
de cóleras, traiciones, esperanzas,
vislumbres repentinos, abandonos,
hambres, gritos de miedo y desamparo
y alegría fulgiendo en las tinieblas
y palabras y amor y amor y amores)
lo cortarán los años.

Nadie verá la destrucción. Ninguno
recogerá la página inconclusa.

Entre el puñado de actos
dispersos, aventados al azar, no habrá uno
al que pongan aparte como a perla preciosa.

Y sin embargo, hermano, amante, hijo,
amigo, antepasado,
no hay soledad, no hay muerte
aunque yo olvide y aunque yo me acabe.

Hombre, donde tú estás, donde tú vives
permanecemos todos.

[From *Lívida luz,* 1960, in *Poesía no eres tú,* 1972]

Presence

Someday I'll know. This body that has been
my dwelling place, my prison, my hospital, is my tomb.

This that I drew together around a dream,
a pain, a memory,
will give way in search of water, the leaf,
the original spore, and even the inert and the stone.

This knot that I was (inextricable
from anger, betrayals, hopes,
sudden glimmers of light, impetuosity,
hunger, cries of fear and helplessness
and joy illuminating the darkness
and words and love and love and loves)
will be cut apart by the years.

No one will see the destruction. None
will gather up the unfinished pages.

Among the handful of disparate acts,
blown about by chance, none will be
set apart like a precious pearl.

And nevertheless, brother, lover, child,
friend, forefather,
there is no solitude, no death
though I may forget and I may come to an end.

Fellowman, wherever you are, wherever you live
there shall we all remain.

Memorial de Tlatelolco

La oscuridad engendra la violencia
y la violencia pide oscuridad
para cuajar en crimen.

Por eso el dos de octubre aguardó hasta la noche
para que nadie viera la mano que empuñaba
el arma, sino sólo su efecto de relámpago.

Y a esa luz, breve y lívida, ¿quién? ¿Quién es el que mata?
¿Quiénes los que agonizan, los que mueren?
¿Los que huyen sin zapatos?
¿Los que van a caer al pozo de una cárcel?
¿Los que se pudren en el hospital?
¿Los que se quedan mudos, para siempre, de espanto?

¿Quién? ¿Quiénes? Nadie. Al día siguiente, nadie.

La plaza amaneció barrida; los periódicos
dieron como noticia principal
el estado del tiempo.
Y en la televisión, en la radio, en el cine
no hubo ningún cambio de programa,
ningún anuncio intercalado ni un
minuto de silencio en el banquete.
(Pues prosiguió el banquete.)

No busques lo que no hay: huellas, cadáveres,
que todo se le ha dado como ofrenda a una diosa:
a la Devoradora de Excrementos.

No hurgues en los archivos pues nada consta en actas.

Tlatelolco Memorial

Darkness engenders violence
and violence seeks darkness
to cover its crime.

And so October the second waited until nightfall
so that no one would see the hand that clutched
the weapon, only the lightning flash of its effect.

And in that light, brief and livid, who? Who is it that kills?
Who are those who suffer, those who die?
Those who flee without shoes?
Those who will fall into the pit of a jail cell?
Those who languish in the hospital?
Those who forever remain silent out of fear?

Who? No one. On the following day, no one.

At dawn the plaza appeared swept clean; the newspapers
gave as their principal news item
the status of the weather.
And on television, on the radio, in the movie houses
there was no change of venue
no interrupting newsflash, not even
a moment of silence at the banquet.
(Of course the banquet went on as planned.)

Do not search for what does not exist: clues, bodies,
for all has been given as an offering to a goddess:
to the Devourer of Excrement.

Do not plunder in the archives, for nothing is recorded.

Ay, la violencia pide oscuridad
porque la oscuridad engendra el sueño
y podemos dormir soñando que soñamos.

Mas he aquí que toco una llaga: es mi memoria.
Duele, luego es verdad. Sangra con sangre.
Y si la llamo mía traiciono a todos.

Recuerdo, recordamos.

Esta es nuestra manera de ayudar que amanezca
sobre tantas conciencias mancilladas,
sobre un texto iracundo, sobre una reja abierta,
sobre el rostro amparado tras la máscara.

Recuerdo, recordemos
hasta que la justicia se siente entre nosotros.

[From *De la tierra de en medio,* in *Poesía no eres tú,* 1972. Originally published in *Siempre!*
in 1968 to commemorate the death of hundreds of students killed by government troops
in Mexico City's Tlatelolco Plaza just prior to the opening of the Olympics.]

Alas, violence seeks darkness
because darkness engenders sleep
and we can sleep dreaming that we dream.

But behold, I touch a wound: it is my memory.
It hurts, therefore it is true. It bleeds real blood.
And yet, if I call it mine, I betray everyone else.

I remember, we all remember.

This is our way of bringing the dawn
to so many stained consciences,
to an impassioned text, to an open window,
to a face shielded behind a mask.

I remember, let us all remember
until justice takes its place among us.

Prose Fiction

I remember, let us all remember
Until justice takes its place among us.
> —Rosario Castellanos,
> "Memorial de Tlatelolco"

We shall whisper the origin.
We shall whisper the story
and the tale, and that is all.
> —El libro de consejo,
> an ancient Maya manuscript

All moons, all years, all days,
all winds, take their course and pass away
Even so all blood reaches its place of quiet,
as it reaches its power and its throne.
> —Chilam-Balam de Chumayel,
> an ancient Maya manuscript

Woe unto them who call evil good and good evil; who put darkness for
light, and light for darkness; who put bitter for sweet and sweet for
bitter.
> —Isaiah 5:20

Rosario Castellanos composed isolated bits of prose along with poetry "from the beginning," though none found its way to print until 1950. The same abstract/concrete, image/idea, lyric/narrative counterpoint that characterizes her poetry is also a dominant note in the development of her prose. She viewed the two genres as complementary and saw in the latter new ways to express her evolving concepts of reality: "I wanted to relate events that were not essential like those of poetry: adjectival happenings."[1]

As in the case of her poetry, Rosario Castellanos's earliest prose works reflect the solitude and isolation of her childhood years. The opening selection, "Three Knots in the Net," was first published in a 1961 cultural periodical of Mexico's National University, where Rosario was then teaching. It passed relatively unnoticed until its reappearance in 1985, in an anthology of Chiapanecan short stories. With clearly autobiographical overtones, it depicts the tragic lives of three members of a provincial family trapped in a net of loneliness and mutual alienation. Though they, like their author, seek meaning and fulfillment in life, they are beset by conflicts from within and without and experience only sadness and disillusion.

The next four pieces are from the Cycle of Chiapas and reveal Castellanos's deep concern for the plight of the Tzeltal-Tzotzil Indians who live there. Through the eyes of her child-narrator in the autobiographical *Balún-Canán* (Nine Guardians), the reader comes face to face with the mythic structure of Chiapas's indigenous culture. The child, who spends far more time with her Indian *nana* than with her own parents, evokes the conflictive, bicultural ambience of Chiapas in lyrical terms that are simple and childlike, yet deeply insightful. As Rosario later explained: "The world in which she moves is so filled with fantasy that poetic images work well. This childlike world is very similar to the mythical world of the Indian where the action of the novel is set."[2]

Castellanos's interpretation of the dichotomized Ladino/Indian cultural reality continues in the next two selections, both short stories from the *Ciudad Real* (Royal City) collection. Less lyric than the reflective *Balún-Canán,* this work reveals its author's evolving commitment to portray the injustices, hopes, and dreams of the local population, this time in clear and direct narrative fashion. Its setting is a Ladino city surrounded by Indian towns and villages, where the two conflicting racial groups live by different sets of realities, but with only one set of laws—the one that protects the Ladino's privileged position and deprives the Indian of any status whatsoever.

The two characters in the first of these stories, "The Luck of Teodoro Méndez Acúbal," personify the respective fear and mutual distrust of the two communities. Their final, tragic confrontation climaxes the counterpointing of their two characters, as they dramatize, in this single incident, the misunderstanding and mistrust that has characterized Indian/Ladino relationships throughout the centuries.

The longer and more complex "Cycle of Hunger" adds a male/female counterpoint to the basic Ladino/Indian one seen in the previous story. These two Ladino protagonists, who have both come to Ciudad Real in an effort to help the Indians, must confront not only the racial prejudices of the area, but also a basic distrust of their motives on the part of the Indians themselves. Further clashes occur as they become enmeshed in the conflict of their individual personalities, as well as the one that is seen in their two contrasting philosophies of social service.

Similar Ladino/Indian, male/female conflicts are seen in the novel fragment that follows. As in *Balún-Canán* and *Ciudad Real, Oficio de tinieblas* (Tenebrae Service) reveals the bitter realities of Chiapanecan life. The Indian remains the victim of Ladino brutality and exploitation, as well as of his own unchanging beliefs and practices. From the legend-like opening lines to the tragedy of the final chapters, the novel presents a world of misunderstanding and violence, made more personal and poignant when seen from the counterpoint perspective of its well-developed and realistic Indian and Ladino characters. All relationships are marred by mistrust and alienation and continue the pattern of dominator/dominated, exploiter/exploited, victimizer/victim seen in the previous two works.

In the collection *Album de familia* (Family Album), from which "Cooking Lesson" is taken, Castellanos leaves behind the world of Chiapas and its Ladino/Indian relationships and focuses instead on the contemporary urban scene. The conflictive male/female dichotomy remains, however, as the author depicts the problematical co-existence between members of the two sexes, compounded by the traditional, preordained roles they are compelled to play out. The resulting effect is dehumanizing for both and creates barriers between them that parallel those of the Ladino/Indian world. Culturally imposed codes of behavior weave a net of entrapment—a recurring metaphor reminiscent of the earlier "three knots"—that stifles and destroys creativity and communion. Though related in a more sophisticated style and in the ironic, humorous vein of Castellanos's later works, the story nevertheless ends on the all-too-familiar note of despair.

By presenting these conflicts in her novels and stories, Rosario Castellanos hoped to provide a literature that could serve as a catalyst for change. Leaving behind her earlier view of the world as an "object of aesthetic contemplation," she came to see it as a "place of struggle" where races and individuals are caught up in an ongoing quest for justice and dignity, a search for "another way to be human and free."

Three Knots in the Net

Agueda's birth caused consternation—half from dismay, half from satisfaction with the fulfillment of prophecy—among the members of the San-román family.

After Juliana's first three consecutive failures at motherhood, it was not only predictable but also just that she give birth to a boy. But who can trust these women from low-class neighborhoods, without lineage or family pride? She had a girl, and if that were not enough, the prudish woman allowed herself the luxury of being unable to conceive again.

Where—they whispered during the Sunday get-togethers, drowsy after abundant feasting—where are Esteban's beautiful cane fields going to end up, his enormous herds of cattle, his farms in both high country and low? Into the hands of some stranger, more than likely. Because Agueda, to all appearances, was not going to be easy to marry off.

Esteban didn't worry too much about his daughter's future. He only calculated that her dowry would have to be greater than what he had originally planned. After all, she was his only child, since the illegitimate ones didn't count. As for Juliana, she was confident that the girl would improve with age. Futhermore, she was going to take it upon herself to make sure her daughter made good use of all the fine points of coquetry. If she did her best to remain chaste and to appear hardworking and good-natured, she wouldn't lack admirers who would want to marry her. After all, like the old saying goes, marriage, like death, is an unalterable state.

But as Agueda grew, her parents' dreams and illusions found less and less cause for affirmation. Esteban's fortune diminished, almost to the point of extinction, when the lands were redistributed by the government and the Indians rebelled, refusing to continue to work without pay. His financial state was neither exceptional nor secret. And now it could be said, without fear of contradiction, that his daughter was turning out to be a little strange.

Who has she taken after, Dear Lord of Esquipulas?

During sleepless nights, in their respective brass beds, Juliana and Esteban recalled the anecdotes of their mutual forebears in hopes of finding the cause, the root, the explanation.

"Maybe that distant cousin of yours, the one from Tabasco, the one that went mad."

"And what should she have done? Carranza's men raped her in front of her boyfriend and later they finished him off with a bullet."

Juliana sighed sympathetically. It was one of the tragedies that clouded her youth and one of which she would like to have been the protagonist. The fact that her husband didn't understand her irritated her. In retaliation she commented:

"And your great-grandmother? They say she used to sleep in a coffin she had made for when her time came."

"Mama Gregoria always took precautions."

"She overdid it."

"On the other hand, there are those who prefer to owe everybody and his brother, with never a thought for the future." Juliana felt the stab of the innuendo. Esteban alluded, of course, to her mother, the widow who never knew —poor thing!—what it was to have a bank account or save a penny. And she hadn't even been able to see her daughters well situated. There was Juliana, for example. Tied down to a man twenty years older and with twenty thousand more bad habits. All he had going for him was the advantage of wealth. And as for her sister . . .

As if her thoughts had converged with her husband's, he asked, with feigned innocence:

"Did you ever find out what caused your sister Elena's death?"

"They didn't poison her to get her inheritance, like they did yours."

What had begun with quiet whisperings was turning into a loud and violent argument. Insults, recriminations, and reproaches ricocheted about the high ceilings, thick walls, and enormous rooms of the house in Comitán.

In the adjacent bedroom, Agueda woke with a start.

"They're talking about me."

She could distinguish her father's voice—solid like his body, solemn like his steps, sharp like the point of the mahogany cane that always indicated promptly the exact place she was to stand. On the other hand, her mother's phrases were like the flowing of a waterfall, giving the impression that nothing could stop her. And suddenly the stammering would start, like when she would scramble through boxes in search of something she'd forgotten. And finally there was total silence.

What Agueda didn't know was that her mother fell silent not because of her husband's reasoning, nor out of prudence, but rather from fear. Not fear of anger or punishment or reprisals. The fear of reconciliation.

Agueda, too, shivered from other terrors: fear of the dark, where ghosts lived, where ferocious beasts lurked. But most of all the fear of those sudden parental voices that kept on covering her with painful wounds—wounds of a guilt whose name she never fully understood, a guilt that rotted her bones, strangled her heart, and resounded like idle words in her head.

Furthermore, a guilt without atonement. Often the child dreamed that she had died and that her empty place had been filled by another, the one who should really have been there all along; and that the breath of air she had previously stolen now gave strength to its rightful owner.

Upon awakening, she never entirely recovered the certainty of being alive. She didn't want to recover it. She would slip without a sound through the hallways—avoiding encounters with mirrors—and hide herself at the far end of the back patio. There she would stay until someone would brusquely retrieve her when it was time to eat.

In the presence of her elders, it was impossible to make her speak, because she was not there.

Esteban and Juliana, for their part, paid attention to nothing but their own hostility and rancor. They asked for the salt with a tone of sarcasm; they thanked each other caustically for the dessert. They wasted not a single superfluous word in conversation.

Agueda would run from the dining room as soon as she could to look for her favorite, far-away refuge. There, as dusk fell, she entertained herself by twisting the fragile necks of birds that flew lower and with less velocity at sunset until they were within easy reach of her rapacious hands. Afterwards, with the small cadaver hidden between her blouse and her chest, Agueda would go to the garden, and in one of the narrow flower beds she would dig a small hole to bury it. On top of the upturned dirt she placed a flower, as a sign of mourning.

She also found pleasure in stripping lizards of their green leather covering. Beneath its rough surface there appeared a whitish, almost transparent membrane that allowed her to see the wild palpitation of its entrails. Agueda watched patiently as the rhythm gradually decreased and then stopped as if paralyzed. Then, with great care, she would place the animal on a rock and set it free. The lizard would remain motionless for an instant and then would run off to lose itself in the underbrush.

Once Juliana surprised the child at her games. Her first impulse was to snatch her up and thrash her soundly to put an end to such cruel deeds. But then a kind of ancestral veneration constrained her. "Agueda is a Sanromán," she said to herself. How was she, Juliana, to rebel against that immutable hierarchy? "She is a Sanromán," she repeated, backing away. Therefore, whatever streak of cruelty or tyranny might be in her was inherited from the ancient tormentors of slaves, the old scourgers of Indians. From her, from the humble embroiderer from San Sebastián, the girl had inherited nothing. Juliana breathed a sigh of relief as she savored her own innocence.

Impunity made Agueda lazy and rebellious. She was unaware of the cause of her parents' weakness towards her, but had proven to herself that neither of the two dared give her an order or reprimand a capricious act of disobedience. "They probably feel sorry for me," she guessed. "And when I say something, they answer me with 'yes, yes,' just like they respond to madmen and to fools."

Juliana sometimes tried to entice her daughter into doing domestic chores by turning them into games. Agueda avoided such traps with the instructive retort:

"That's the servants' job."

At times, however, she would condescend to water the plants or sweep some corner, until an attack of sneezing kept her from continuing the task. And the only time she entered the kitchen she fainted from revulsion at the sight of the raw food.

When Juliana tried to begin adorning her daughter with all the graces a young lady should have, she encountered an awkwardness so obstinate as to be regarded as depraved. On the keyboard of the piano she was unable to distinguish the sound of one note from another, and if she put her fingers down wrong at the beginning, the whole lesson went badly. She would sew and unravel pieces of cloth that never were made into anything useful. And as for painting, she never got past scribbling on papers that she would later discard with contempt.

"She can never be left alone," Juliana thought. But friendships didn't come easy either. Because of her family's position and social class, she belonged to a predetermined and select circle from the moment of her birth. She was welcomed, but soon they began to avoid her with one pretext or another. Why be with someone who was bored with all the games? Because Agueda didn't like to make mudpies or change doll diapers or make friends with any of them.

She had to rely on *cargadoras* and pay these Indian children special prices, in spite of the fact that they would run away at the slighest provocation. Actually, they were frightened by the passivity with which Agueda let them entertain her. Songs, dances, stories, everything that could be observed from afar without her having to participate. And the poor servants could never predict the moment when Agueda would hurl herself at them, tearing at their ears because they had not precisely answered one of her questions.

"This is going too far," her mother decided. "She must be in league with the devil."

And she went to consult with her spiritual advisor.

This man with his Roman profile and moving pulpit voice, an idol of the people, advised her:

"Bring her to me. We must get to the root of the evil that is tormenting her. I will train her in doctrine myself."

Juliana enjoyed a fleeting moment of triumph. Her sisters-in-law were overcome with envy. The priest would never have agreed to do the same for anyone but Agueda.

With Father Ripalda's catechism in one hand and a rod in the other, the classes in the parochial parlor began. The questions were easy, quick, mechanical. That's how the answers should have been. But Agueda, after meditating with furrowed brow, would come up with a new question, with the application of a rule to a concrete case that resulted in the opposite conclusion, demanding that the meanings be clarified so as not to lead to mistakes, and with endless doubts.

The priest would let his arms drop by his sides. The catechism was not explicit enough and the rod was unjust. He spoke to Doña Juliana in private, confiding to her that her daughter's case was so unusual that he dared not give her the sacrament for fear of committing a sacrilege.

What was to be done in the face of such dishonor, which her sisters-in-law immediately undertook to spread throughout the town? Get away from there, to some place where no one knew them, where no one would point at them in mocking pity. To Mexico City.

Once in the capital, Juliana was unable to find a way to keep Agueda from clinging to her skirt tails. How could she let her roam the streets to be run over by a car in some moment of distraction? How could she enroll her in public school to fend for herself among the hoards of insolent, unruly school children? Because, thank God, Agueda would be everything they wanted her to be. But malicious—no.

And so, there was no alternative but to find a school run by nuns, a very fine one with a good reputation, and above all, expensive. Yes, the most expensive one. That was the ultimate guarantee.

When Esteban arrived in Mexico City after liquidating all his assets in Chiapas, he found his family already settled in.

The surprise was not a pleasant one. The apartment that Juliana had rented was exceedingly small, and the furniture was second-hand. What's more, there were no servants, since they had to be sacrificed to pay the school fees.

Esteban approved of all of the hidden virtues in each of Juliana's decisions. But he was overcome by nostalgia when he remembered his fiber hammock in the corridor, the open spaces that before he took for granted, the air that no longer smelled warmly of fritters and burning trash.

The reason for all this upheaval was Agueda, and it was not going to be easy for Esteban to forgive her. But when he saw her returning from school in her gray uniform, with her heavy knapsack and, for the first time, an eager, alert air about her, he hardly recognized her.

"She gets very good grades," Juliana boasted. "Would you like to see them?"

Agueda was already opening her book satchel when her father's negative gesture immobilized her. She stood there perplexed, looking at him. How incongruent was the figure of this stranger into whose arms she had been about to jump! How absurd he seemed in his vest and gold watch-chain, with his mahogany cane and greenish hat!

Without a word, they went into the dining room. Juliana bustled about noisily in the kitchen and arrived with a pot of steaming soup full of stew meat and frijoles. Agueda barely ate, and Esteban picked at a bit of this and that, complaining because it was not well seasoned, or that it was too hot and burned his mouth, or that it had lost its flavor when it got cold.

Juliana sat down at the end of the table and folded her hands, red from lye and hard work, on the sheet of plastic that served as a tablecloth. Here next to her were the two people to whom she was inextricably bound, by obligation and unalterable family ties. As if illuminated by a lightning flash, she contemplated them like strangers, from afar. She had never understood them or even loved them. This last revelation disturbed her. And to exorcise it she mentally prayed a series of short prayers.

The days took on an invariable routine. Agueda and Juliana would awaken early so the girl could get to school on time. Around midday Esteban, dressed in his Sunday best, would march off downtown, where he was working on some vague business matter he never bothered to explain. He had influential friends; it was only a matter of time before he would receive his appointment.

This rendition was accurate for a while. Then, after long and fruitless hours spent in waiting rooms, Esteban decided to spend his mornings in a more pleasant place. He chose the Alameda Park. He would look for a bench that suited him and ceremoniously unfold his newspaper. On certain occasions, to celebrate some especially important event, Esteban would stretch his legs to the rapid beat of a *bolero* melody.

At times he would chat with some other person who frequented the place, but he never allowed the conversation to go beyond the limits of weather or political observations. Thus he maintained his distance, as well as his rapidly diminishing dignity. First he had to dispense with his cane, too cumbersome to contend with when riding on public transports. Then one day while he was napping on the streetcar en route home, a thief snatched his hat. As a precaution, he put away his watch and chain, leaving his vest with only the shine of age and continuous use.

In his daily absences Juliana sensed an adventure.

"This is not to be tolerated, even from God the Father," she repeated, furiously scrubbing away at her pots and pans.

At night, and for the most trivial of pretexts, the fight would begin. Vulgar words, vile adjectives burst from her lips. Agueda began to count the time that would lapse between the rage and the repentance that came afterward. Esteban prolonged it by refusing to respond to any of her accusations, sheltered behind the classified ads of his newspaper.

At dawn (Juliana was an insomniac) she would quietly tiptoe to her husband's bed to ask forgiveness. Esteban turned his face to the wall and, as if in a dream, repeated over and over: "too late . . . too late. . . ."

This was the beginning of the silence. The three were always absorbed in their own projects, their own daily happenings, their own memories. None of them had a thing to share with anyone else.

Juliana at first believed that doing her own housework was just a temporary measure. But Esteban considered the situation satisfactory and definitive. He liked to watch her wax the floors, wash the windows, make the beds, from the vantage point of a special armchair he had acquired for his own exclusive use.

Now she's making up for all those years of idleness in Comitán. After all, what else could she have become but a servant, without my name and my money?

His money.

His money. With it he had once acquired youth and beauty, a pretense of love that had faded. With it he had permanently assured himself of Juliana's fidelity and self-denial. He considered it his only instrument of dominion, the only backbone that kept him erect and above those around him. For this reason he clung to it desperately, so as not to let it slip through his fingers.

Each morning he waited for the moment when his wife would ask him for it. He watched her hesitation at the threshold, her pretense at looking for something near his armchair, her diligent dusting of the surface of an adjacent piece of furniture. At last the phrase would slip, stifled and trembling, from Juliana's lips. Esteban pretended not to hear her, and she would be forced to repeat her plea. Moved by anguish, Juliana now spoke clearly and distinctly.

"I need ten pesos to do the shopping."

Esteban would look at her with an air of infinite compassion. Had she suddenly gone mad? Money can't be swept up on the streets to be squandered in such a way.

"What do you want it for?"

"For groceries."

"Is this for some special banquet? Are we having guests so you can show off by serving pheasant or stuffed turkey?"

Without a trace of humor or impatience, as if the interrogation were normal, Juliana responded:

"Everything is very expensive nowadays."

"The paper says that the steps they're taking to cut the cost of living are showing magnificent results."

"If you don't believe me, go with me to the plaza."

"How can you think I don't believe you? You're my wife, and a wife should never lie to her husband."

"Then give me the ten pesos."

"But first, explain to me: what are you going to buy?"

"Fifty grams of rice."

"Isn't that too much? Yesterday more than half of the soup was left over."

"It's not wasted. We'll have it for supper later."

"Well, here's the money for the rice. What else?"

"Half a kilo of meat."

"Half a kilo! Why don't you just buy a whole cow?"

"You eat most of it. Agueda and I barely touch it."

"Choose it carefully, then. Tender, not stringy. Only the best cuts. Is that all?"

"We need vegetables and frijoles."

"You can't deny that those are cheap."

"No."

"Then seven pesos should be enough. Here."

"But you're forgetting the fruit and the sweets and the coffee."

"If you knew how to shop wisely, it could all come out of this." As if she hadn't heard him, Juliana insisted:

"I need to buy soap and sugar, too."

"But you bought some just last week."

"We're out again."

"I don't understand, unless they're not giving you the right measure at the store."

"Maybe."

"Well, demand it. You have the right."

Juliana made a final gesture of agreement and thrust out her hand for the other three pesos that Esteban handed her magnanimously. Immediately afterward, her hurried steps could be heard as she made her way toward the street. And the sound of the door as it closed behind her.

Agueda interrupted her school work to watch the two protagonists of the scene. Avarice, servility. Was this what marriage was all about? No, surely not. She was certain that her schoolmates' parents lived differently. They loved each other.

She thought about this word without the slightest notion of its meaning. She had never loved anyone, much less this strange pair of stingy, vulgar beings from whom she had never been able to free herself. Everyone assured her that Esteban and Juliana were her parents, but she rejected this affirmation with all her might. The whole world was lying to hide who knows what infamous plan. One day her real parents, the ones who had given her life in an act of selflessness and joy, would come to rescue her from this hell.

She contented herself with imagining how they might be. He was refined and was beginning to age with dignity. He had traveled, was well-read. He held a very important position, and his time was spent in meaningful and noteworthy activities. But when he returned home he was just a simple, affectionate man who respected her mother and pampered their daughter.

As for her mother, she was charming. Tall, very elegant, with her hair softly pulled back. And her face, untouched by make-up, was serene and sweet.

When they came to claim Agueda, neither Esteban nor Juliana would dare stop them. They would let her go to a luxurious house, where each detail revealed the care and good taste of its owners.

The first nights they wouldn't sleep.

They had so many things to share! Later, when Agueda had finished her schooling, with awards for excellence, they would reward her with a trip to the most beautiful European cities. When she returned, HE would be there waiting for her—an industrious young man who worked alongside her father. Everyone predicted a magnificent future for her. . . .

Agueda was abruptly brought back to reality. The door had closed with a slam. It was Juliana returning from the market, out of breath, her face flushed.

The year Agueda finished high school there was a ceremony at the close of the school year. All the graduates were to attend, in cap and gown, to receive their diplomas. The parents would sit in the audience to applaud their daughters' crowning achievements.

Agueda decided, from the very first, not to tell Esteban and Juliana about it. To keep them from attending, she pretended to be sick and didn't recover until after the event had passed.

The incident would have gone unnoticed except for the zeal of the school principal, who sent a message to Juliana requesting an interview.

Juliana became nervous. She begged Esteban to go in her place, but he steadfastly refused. So she had no choice but to search the closet for her least out-of-style dress—the one that seemed most appropriate for the occasion. One of her neighbors provided a pair of gloves, and another a hat and purse that didn't match. The problem of shoes could not be solved, so she had to wear her everyday ones.

Juliana felt lightheaded in this unaccustomed finery. And the sensation grew worse as she crossed the immense silence of the vacant courtyards. When she reached the waiting room, she was overwhelmed with nausea, bathed in a cold sweat.

After a quick glance in Juliana's direction, the principal invited her to sit down. She herself remained standing behind her desk, its only ornament an iron crucifix.

"I consider it my duty, madam, to talk to you about your daughter Agueda. Of course we can't fault her in any way concerning her dedication to her studies. It is a gift the Lord has given her and she doesn't misuse it. But there is something about her that has always disturbed me: her conduct."

Juliana remembered the twisted necks of the birds, the flayed lizards, and felt a shiver that did not deter her interlocutor.

"It's not that she is undisciplined. On the contrary. She obeys the rules to a degree that I would call exaggerated. But there is no enthusiasm, no feeling in anything she does; rather a kind of cruelty, as if in fulfilling her tasks she were destroying an obstacle or avenging herself of something . . . of someone."

"Forgive my lack of understanding, Mother, but what you are telling me is so strange. . . ."

"I am unaware of Agueda's attitude at home, with her family. But here, in all the years she was among us, she never made friends with any of her class-mates. She never established one of those admirable bonds with any of her teachers. Nor was she ever caught up in one of those whims so common to adolescents. She didn't even choose a regular confessor. She was indifferent in going to one priest or another. And when she was ordered to persevere, she obeyed without protest."

"She's always been very cold, very indifferent with everyone."

"What I'm not sure about is whether it's a question of character or of the treatment she has received from those who should show her the most atten-tion, the most affection. Why didn't she come to the graduation ceremony? She knew she was to receive her diploma and several awards."

"When was it? We knew nothing about it."

"It doesn't matter now. But that confirms my suspicions. Agueda didn't come because she knew no one would accompany her to this solemn and unique occasion. Perhaps attending by herself would have caused her too much pain."

Mechanically Juliana began to remove the gloves that painfully squeezed her hands. What is this woman talking about? And she doesn't let up; she just goes on and on. . . .

"I understand why your husband couldn't miss his daily obligations. But you, madam, couldn't you have given up some appointment, possibly a trivial one, when your daughter needed you to be with her?"

Suddenly Juliana understood the truth. Agueda had hidden everything from them deliberately, because she wanted neither Esteban nor her to attend the ceremony with all her classmates' parents present. She kept them away because she was ashamed of them.

Juliana had suspected it many times, in small details. When she and Agueda would walk down the street together, the girl would go ahead as if to disguise her relationship to the shabby woman who was struggling painfully to keep up with her. She was always willing to sacrifice any outing, any amusement, if her parents were planning to go along. And now she had chosen to miss the graduation celebration to avoid having to introduce them.

The evidence was so clear that Juliana felt an enormous relief. Finally she had sufficient reason to grant Agueda the freedom to go out alone or with whomever she thought worthy of her own company! How nice it would be to stay at home with her apron on and her hair down, shuffling around in her old slippers while the radio played her favorite song.

Her daughter was at a dangerous age now, filled with expectations and temptations. If she couldn't confide in her mother, whom could she trust?

No, not a song. One of those new soap operas would be better. If she didn't hurry, she'd miss it. Quickly Juliana stood up, and without hesitating to see if the principal's speech was coming to an end, she walked toward her and took her hand to kiss it.

"Thank you, Mother. Thank you for everything."

The contact, although fleeting, with Juliana's hands—calloused and cracked by lye—made the principal reconsider her previous opinion. No, the woman who just left here was neither a social butterfly nor a clever canasta player. As for her appearance, when she thought about it, it seemed depressing at best. Was Agueda's family poor? But they had never gotten behind in paying their bills. At any rate, it was for the best that she had completed her studies. Crossing herself before the crucifix and making an act of reverence, the principal also left the room.

On the way back to her apartment, in the cool, remote March sunlight,

Juliana removed her hat and loosened her hair to let the breeze blow through it freely. She didn't feel ashamed or sad about what she had just experienced. She simply thought once more: Agueda is a Sanromán. And so she was justified in despising her. And the curious thing is that her contempt made her feel frivolous, unburdened, free. Within her she felt pity for her husband, who was probably worrying now about Agueda's future. He didn't realize that it was not necessary to do so—that the girl was stronger and more merciless than anyone.

At suppertime, the only time Esteban assumed his role as head of the house, he launched into a lengthy harangue on the advantages of a career in pharmacy. It was most appropriate for a young lady, he reasoned. And as soon as she earned her diploma, she could easily make good money by merely letting some pharmacy (that wanted to have a responsible person up front) hang it on the wall.

Agueda agreed to everything. What her father said was true. But she had just completed her application to Law School.

Some hidden instinct prompted her in that direction without consulting anyone. She concluded that familiarity with the law could provide a justification for her existence—an existence whose value had been questionable since her birth. It could also give her future a valid course and calm her anxieties and doubts.

When her decision was casually revealed, Esteban adopted the grave air of a defenseless, wounded victim. He didn't speak to Agueda again except to allude to the ingratitude of children, to their lack of respect for the experience and advice of their elders, and to the fact that death was to be preferred over reaching the point of being a bother.

Agueda listened to him with rapt attention, as if it were up to her to classify the species of this man who had reached old age without ever experiencing any sort of love or understanding. At last she filed him under a derogatory name and paid no further attention to his laments.

With it all, a semblance of peace and harmony prevailed in the house, at least enough of one for Juliana to feel comfortable. She gave up (it was about time!) all her efforts to look presentable. She threw her girdle in the trash and bought herself some house dresses at the market.

Her free time increased when Agueda got a job at a law firm and began to eat downtown. In this way she was able to devote herself, accompanied by her indispensable radio, to the embroidery of the interminable tablecloth she planned to donate to the church in Comitán, as an act of thanksgiving for blessings received and as a plea that her luck not change.

Her luck did change, however, and very abruptly.

One night, Esteban awoke with a sharp pain in his chest, in his left arm, and in his side.

The doctor diagnosed probable angina pectoris, prescribed several medicines, and recommended that he get plenty of rest.

It was then that Esteban Sanromán achieved what he thought he would never have in life: happiness. From that point on, he didn't have to invent business appointments or waste his mornings sweltering or freezing, depending on the season, on an uncomfortable bench in the park. Now his armchair was his throne. Comfortably reclining, he could now devote himself to the careful monitoring of his heartbeat, the rhythm of his pulse, the sudden heaving of his chest.

In the face of this new emergency, Juliana took refuge in the sacraments, in order to strengthen her faith and bear her cross with resignation.

She provided her husband with every imaginable comfort: cushions, blankets for his legs, magazines and games to keep him entertained—from a simple deck of cards to the complexities of chess. Agueda came and went, to her classes and her job, and always found the couple so totally absorbed in endless, frenzied competition that she found it disgusting.

Juliana would also surprise her husband with delicate, light snacks.

The result of all her efforts was a growing warmth between the two. But when Juliana tried to measure its depth she immediately encountered that attitude so peculiar to the Sanrománs, which meant: everything that others do for me, they do out of duty and because I deserve it; whatever I receive is merely what rightfully belongs to me.

This disappointment, and perhaps her fatigue, made Juliana begin to distance herself from her ailing husband. He would complain in vain about his wife's rebellion and how shabbily she treated him. How dare she, for example, hire a servant to wait on him without even asking his permission?

"Because I need to go out once in a while, and I don't want to leave you alone."

Go out? Such a thing was unheard of!

"Out shopping?" her husband would ask, threateningly.

"I like to go window shopping. And every now and then I see a movie. I've got to find amusement somewhere, don't I?"

"Oh, sure," Esteban responded, his teeth clenched in resentment. "Since you are strong and able, go on and do it. Meanwhile I'll just rot here."

His words had not the slightest effect on Juliana's plans. She already had her coat on and was checking her purse one final time to make sure she hadn't forgotten anything important.

Her absences, since they were so often repeated, soon became habit. And each time they grew longer. But she didn't seem happy when she returned. Instead, her expression became increasingly sad and dejected.

Some mornings she lingered until the last minute before getting out of bed. Then, after two or three steps, she would collapse again, exhausted.

Esteban observed all these symptoms with secret satisfaction. Maybe now Juliana would see what it was like to be sick and helpless.

"I think I need a vacation," Juliana said, turning to Esteban after a prolonged examination of her ashen, emaciated image in the mirror.

"You know we don't have money to throw away like that."

"Don't worry. I have a cousin in Tehuacán. She owns a guest house. If I help her out some, she won't charge me room and board."

"And what about me? I'm not going to stay here at the mercy of some ignorant servant."

"A nurse will come take care of you."

"Looks like you're determined to ruin me."

"She's a nun. She does it out of charity."

There was nothing more to discuss. Besides, Juliana's bag was already packed. The only thing left to do was say good-bye to Agueda.

She entered her daughter's bedroom as she was undressing.

"You know I'm going away for a few days."

"I heard something like that."

"I wanted to leave you a little something. In case you need anything."

Juliana placed a thick roll of bills on a small table. Agueda stared at it, speechless.

"Did you steal it from my father?"

Juliana shrugged her shoulders as if the deed had no significance.

"Spend it. At your age there are lots of things you want to buy."

The next morning Agueda and Juliana went out together to wait for the taxi. The servant came behind them, carrying her suitcase.

As she opened the door of the cab, Juliana sighed loudly.

"What's wrong?" Agueda asked, perplexed.

"Oh nothing. I'm just clumsy. I bumped into something."

Juliana waited until the vehicle had gone a few blocks before giving the driver the address.

"To the Cancer Institute, please."

The driver took her there without a word. He knew his way to that building. He had taken passengers there many times before.

Juliana paid the driver and refused to let anyone help her with her suitcase.

"It isn't heavy," she explained.

When she reached the information desk she thrust a piece of paper at the woman in charge. After reading it, the woman stated matter-of-factly:

"The terminal patients are on the eighth floor."

"Thank you."

Juliana picked up her suitcase, and with a steady, determined step, she walked toward the elevator.

From Balún-Canán (*The Nine Guardians*)

"And then in anger they dispossessed us, they confiscated what we had held most dear: the word, which is memory's treasure chest. Ever since those days they burn and are consumed with the firewood of the hearth. The smoke rises with the wind and is seen no more. Only the ash remains, and it has no face. All so that you may come, and the one who is younger than you; and a breath, just a breath may suffice you. . . ."

"Don't tell me that story, Nana."

"And so you think I was talking to you? Do you suppose one speaks with anise seeds?"

I'm not an anise seed. I'm a little girl and I'm seven years old. All five fingers of my right hand and two of my left. And when I stand up straight I can see my father's knees just in front of me. But no higher. I suppose he keeps on growing like a great tree with a small tiger hiding in its topmost branches. My mother is different. Birds wander through her hair—so thick and black and curly—and linger there. Or at least that's what I imagine. I've never seen it. I can only see what's at my eye level. Some bushes with their leaves nibbled by insects, the desks stained with ink, my brother. I can see my brother from head to foot, because he was born after me, and when he was born I already knew lots of things that I can tell him about now in great detail. This for example:

"Columbus discovered America."

Mario looks at me as if I'm not worthy of his attention and shrugs his shoulders with indifference. I am choked with rage. Once again, all the weight of injustice falls on me.

"Don't wiggle so, child. How can I finish combing your hair?"

I wonder if my Nana knows that I hate her when she combs my hair? Probably not. She doesn't know much of anything. She's an Indian, she goes barefoot, and she wears no undergarments under her *tzec*.[1] She's not ashamed. She says that the ground doesn't have eyes.

"All done! Now for some breakfast."

But eating is horrible. There in front of me the plate staring back at me without blinking an eye. Then the long expanse of table. After that . . . I don't know. I'm afraid there might be a mirror on the other side.

"Drink up your milk."

Every afternoon at five a Swiss cow goes by tinkling her little tin bell. (I've explained to Mario that Swiss means fat.) Her owner leads her along, tied by a rope, and at every corner he stops and milks her. The servants come out of the houses and buy cupfuls of it. And naughty children like me make faces and spill it on the tablecloth.

"God will punish you for wasting it," Nana tells me.

"I want some coffee. Like you. Like everyone else."

"You'll turn into an Indian."

Her threat frightens me. Beginning tomorrow there'll be no more spilt milk.

4

Whenever the Indians from the ranch at Chactajal come to our house a fiesta is sure to follow. They bring bags of corn and beans, bundles of salt beef, and cakes of brown sugar. Then the granary will be opened and its rats will run about again, fat and sleek.

Lounging in the hammock on the porch, my father receives the Indians. They approach one by one, and offer their foreheads for him to touch with the three middle fingers of his right hand. Then they return to their places at an appropriate distance. My father talks with them about ranch business. He knows their language and their ways. They answer respectfully, in words of one syllable, and laugh briefly when it is necessary.

I go to the kitchen where Nana is heating coffee. "They brought bad news, like the black butterflies." I sniff in the pantry. I like the color of the butter and the feel of the fruit, and I like to peel the skin from the onions. "They are witches' doings, child. They devour everything—crops, peace in the family, people's health."

I have found a basket of eggs. The speckled ones are turkeys'.

"Look what they are doing to me."

And lifting her *tzec,* Nana shows me a tender, reddish wound that disfigures her knee.

I look at it with eyes wide with surprise.

"Don't say anything, child. I came here from Chactajal so they wouldn't follow me. But their evil reaches far."

"Why do they hurt you?"

"Because I was brought up in your house. Because I love your parents and Mario and you."

"Is it bad to love us?"

"It is bad to love those who give orders, those who have possessions. That's what the law says."

The pot rests quietly on the coals. Inside, the coffee has begun to boil.

"Tell them to come now. Their drink is ready."

I go out saddened by what I have just learned. My father bids the Indians farewell with a gesture and remains in his hammock, reading. Now I see him for the first time. It is he who gives orders, he who has possessions. And I can't bear to look at his face, and I run to hide in the kitchen. The Indians are sitting near the fire, holding their steaming cups with great care. Nana serves them with measured courtesy, as if they were kings. On their feet they wear rope sandals—and cakes of mud. Their muslin pants are patched and dirty, and their food bags are empty.

When she finishes serving them, Nana sits down too. Solemnly she stretches both hands toward the fire and holds them there a few moments. They talk, and it is as if they draw a circle about them. In my anguish I break it.

"Nana, I'm cold."

As she has done since I was born, Nana draws me onto her lap. It is warm and caring. But it has a wound, a wound that we have caused.

12

In Comitán we have several fairs every year, but none is as joyous and lively as that of Saint Caralampio. He has the reputation of being a miracle worker, and people make pilgrimages from far away to pray before his image. It was carved in Guatemala and shows him in a kneeling position, with a long white beard and a saintly glow, while the executioner has the fatal ax poised over his head. (All we know about the executioner is that he was a Jew.) But now the people of the village have to stop outside the doors of the church, since it is closed like all the rest, on orders from the government. That isn't sufficient reason to call off the fair, so in the plaza booths and promenades are being set up.

Peddlers come down from San Cristóbal with their load of goods: dried fruit, pickles, badly made rag dolls with their cheeks scandalously painted red to leave no doubt that they are from the cool highlands, pottery shepherds with thick ankles, little sheep made of cotton, boxes of varnished wood, and rustic weavings.

The merchants—all wrapped up in woolen blankets—spread their wares on rush mats on the ground. They proclaim them to the multitudes with voices hoarse from smoking strong tobacco. They haggle patiently and stubbornly over prices. The rancher in his bright satin jacket gapes in astonishment at the abundance spread before him. After thinking long and hard he pulls a home-spun handkerchief from his pocket, unties the knots that guard his money, and buys a pound of hazelnuts, a bundle of cigars, and a small violin. Down the way the lottery is being held:

"The polar-star of the North."

People search their cards, and when they find it they mark the square with a grain of corn.

"Aunt Cleta's umbrella."

The prizes glisten on their shelves. Glass objects of uncertain shapes, rings that have the special virtue of turning everything they touch green, scarves so delicate that at the slightest breeze they blow away like the down of a thistle.

"Doleful death."

"Lottery!"

There is excitement everywhere. Everyone envies the lucky man, who smiles complacently while the dispenser of prizes invites him to choose from all that wealth the thing he fancies most.

Nana and I have been sitting here for hours, and we haven't won anything yet. I am sad, feeling so far removed from the gifts. Nana gets up and says:

"Stay here. I won't be gone long."

I watch her go. She gestures to the man in the booth, and they speak briefly in hushed voices. She hands him something, and he bows as if in gratitude. Then she returns and sits beside me once more.

"Don Ferruco on parade."

I can't find him on my card. But Nana picks up a grain of corn and puts it on one of the pictures.

"Is that Don Ferruco?"

"That's him."

I had no idea that he was a piece of fruit.

"The mandolin from Paris."

Another picture escapes me.

"The heart of a woman."

"Lottery!" Nana cries while the lottery man applauds enthusiastically.

"Which prize do you want?" he asks me.

I choose a ring because I want a green finger.

We go walking through the crowd. People step on our toes and shove us about. High above my head their words and laughter float. There is a smell of cheap perfume in the air, of clothes just ironed, of musty liquor. Chicken in rich chocolate sauce boils in enormous clay pots, and punch spiced with cinnamon is kept bubbling on the fire. In another corner of the plaza they have erected a platform and covered it with fresh cypress for the dance. There are couples embracing in the Ladino fashion, while the marimba plays its rich, dreamy music.

But this year the Fair Organization Commission has done a superb job. They had something brought from town, from the capital itself, that few had seen before: a Ferris wheel. There it stands, huge and resplendent with its thousands of electric lights. Nana and I want to take a ride, but there are so many people in line we have to wait for our turn. In front of us is an Indian. When he gets to the gate he asks for a ticket.

"What do you think of this uppity Indian—standing here speaking Spanish? Who gave you permission to do that?"

Because there are rules. Spanish is our privilege, and we use it speaking "usted" to our superiors, "tú" to our equals, and "vos" to the Indians!

"You insolent Indian, get on in and hold onto your hat."

The Indian takes his ticket without a word.

"Get yourself a drink and stop drooling."

"An upstart Indian's on the Ferris wheel!"

"It's the antichrist!"

They seat us in a kind of cradle-chair. The man running the machine secures the bar that holds us in. He backs away and starts the motor. Slowly we begin to go up, and for an instant we are suspended there. Comitán, the whole town, is in our hands like a nest full of chicks! The dark, moss-covered roofs. The whitewashed walls. The stone towers. And the endless plains. And the swamp. And the wind.

Soon we begin to gain speed. The wheel spins dizzily. Faces are images mingled together, and then we hear a cry of horror from the crowd watching below. At first we are unable to tell what is happening. Then we realize that the bar on the Indian's seat has come unfastened and he has been thrown forward. But he manages to catch hold of the dangling bar, and there he clings as the wheel continues to go round and round.

The attendant turns off the electrical current, but the wheel continues to turn from its own momentum. When at last it comes to a stop, the poor Indian remains aloft, hanging there sweating from exhaustion and fear.

Little by little, so slowly that to our anguished eyes it seemed an eternity, the Indian climbs down. When he is close enough to the ground, he jumps. His face is ashen. Someone offers him a bottle of wine, but he refuses it ungratefully.

"Why did you stop?" he asks.

The man who runs the Ferris wheel is furious.

"What do you mean 'why'? Because you fell and were about to kill yourself, you crazy Indian."

The Indian looks at him, clenching his teeth angrily.

"I didn't fall. I undid the bar. I like riding that way better."

An explosion of laughter greeted his words.

"Would you listen to him!"

"What a fellow!"

The Indian can feel the hate and scorn all around him. He keeps the challenge going.

"I want another ticket. I'll go however I like. And you can't keep me from it."

The onlookers are intrigued by what is about to happen. They whisper and laugh and wink at one another, covering their mouths with their hands.

Nana pushes her way through them, dragging me along, as I turn to look at the place we have left behind. I can't tell what's going on and I complain. She keeps pressing her way through the crowd, in spite of my protests, as quickly as if the hounds were after her. I want to ask her why. But the question catches in my throat when I see that her eyes are filled with tears.

19

Yesterday the supplies arrived for our journey to the ranch at Chactajal. The animals are resting in the stable. They all awoke with their manes and tails braided and curled. And the servants say that last night they heard the jangle of silver spurs on the cobblestone streets. It was the Sombrerón, the ghost that haunts the fields and towns, leaving on the foreheads of animals its signs of evil omen.

Not long ago my cousin Ernesto came to leave his bags. Only three changes of clothes. He wrapped them in an ordinary rush mat and tied them with a rope.

Nana won't go with us to the ranch. She's afraid of the witches. But she has taken charge of getting together the things we'll need for our trip. Early this morning she sent for the woman who grinds chocolate. There they were together, weighing the cocoa and measuring out the sugar and the other ingredients to mix with it. Then the woman went into the room they had prepared especially for her, and before closing the door she warned:

"Nobody must come in while I am working. For there are those who have a burning eye and who cast evil spells wherever they go. And then the chocolate curdles."

On the other hand, the woman who makes candles doesn't keep her work secret. She is in the middle of the patio, right in the sun. She melts the wax in a huge copper cauldron and sings as she hangs the wicks on the nail-laden wheel. Then with a big ladle she pours the melted wax from the pot onto the tapers. With each turn of the wheel more wax adheres to the wicks, and the candles begin to take shape.

In the clay oven the servants are baking bread. It comes out a golden color, covered with a slightly darker crust, smelling of abundance, of blessings, and of riches. They place it in huge baskets, packing it carefully so it doesn't crumble and covering it with white napkins stiff with starch. . . .

The house is a beehive of sounds and activity. Only the Indians are quiet, squatting on their haunches on the veranda, scratching for fleas. My mother can't bear to see them idle, but there's nothing for them to do at the moment. Then she has an idea:

"Look . . . whatever your name is. You go to Señorita Amalia Domínguez's house. She needs a donkey boy to fetch water. And you there, ask someone where Don Jaime Rovelo's house is. He needs somebody to weed his patio."

The Indians get to their feet in their docile way. They sling their foodbags over their shoulders—with their balls of *posol*[2] and toasted cakes—all they have brought with them from the ranch. For they know that where they're going they won't be given anything to eat either.

20

Nana takes me aside to say goodbye. We are in the chapel. We kneel down before the images on the altar.

Then Nana makes the sign of the cross on my forehead and says:

"I come to deliver my little child to Thee, Lord. Thou knowest that I can no longer keep watch over her, as much distance will come between us. But Thou who art everywhere protect her. Clear her pathways so she doesn't trip and fall, so that the stones don't turn and hurt her, so that wild beasts don't spring out and devour her, so that the lightning doesn't burn the roof that shelters her. For through my heart she has come to know Thee and has vowed to be faithful and has worshipped Thee. For Thou art all powerful, for Thou art strong.

"Have mercy on her eyes, that they not look about her like the eyes of a bird of prey.

"Have mercy on her hands, that they not close like a tiger's on his prey, that they be open to give what they possess and to receive what they need, as in obedience to Thy law.

"Have mercy on her tongue, that it not speak threateningly, as the knife sends forth sparks flying when it is sharpened.

"Purify her innermost being, that from it may come, not creeping vines, but great trees that give shelter and bear fruit.

"Keep her, as up to now I have kept her, from speaking scorn. Should anyone come and bow before her, let her not vaunt herself and say: I have bowed the neck of this colt. May she stoop to pick that precious flower—that few in this world are allowed to gather—which is called humility.

"Thou hast granted her servants. Grant her also the spirit of an elder sister, a keeper, a guardian. Grant her the scales on which to weigh her actions, so that she may value patience more than wrath, mercy more than justice, love more than vengeance.

"Open her understanding. Deepen it so that truth may find a place there, that she may pause before discharging the whip, knowing that each lash that falls leaves its mark on the shoulders of its executioner. And may all her gestures be as ointment poured into wounds.

"I come to deliver my child to Thee. I give her to Thee. I commend her to Thee, so that all her days, as one carries jugs of water to the river to be filled, Thou mayest carry her heart into the presence of the good she has received from her servants, so that she may never be found wanting in gratitude, so that she may sit down at a table where hunger has never sat, that she may bless the beautiful cloth that covers it, that she may feel the walls of her dwelling true and solid about her. This is our blood and our work and our sacrifice."

On the porch we hear the coming and going of the mule drivers, of the servants helping to close the trunks. The horses are already saddled and are pawing at the bricks near the door. I hear my mother's voice calling my name, searching for me. Nana gets to her feet. Then she turns to me saying:

"It's time for us to say goodbye, child."

But I stay on the floor clinging to her *tzec,* weeping because I don't want to go.

She pulls away from me gently and raises me up to her face. She kisses my cheeks and makes the sign of the cross on my mouth.

"You see, what with all my praying, it's as if I'd gone back again to the days when I nursed you."

21

When we leave Comitán the sun is already high in the sky. Father and Ernesto ride ahead on horseback. Mother, my brother, and I ride in sedan chairs carried by Indians. We go along at the pace set by the slowest. The sun shines through the canopy stretched over our heads, made of Guatemalan cloth. The air is thick and hot under the canopy and suffocates us.

It takes us a long time to cross the plains. And when they end, the mountains rise before us with their hundred jagged peaks and rugged paths. I measure our altitude by the panting of the Indian who is carrying me. At the height where we are there are also pines. They catch the wind in their many-fingered hands and release it once more anointed with rich resins. Among the rocks grows a sturdy blue flower that gives off a sharp scent of pollen where the bee buzzes drunkenly. The earth is porous and black.

Somewhere up in the mountains the lightning flashes. As if summoned by a shepherd's whistle, the dark wooly clouds flock together over our heads. My father shouts an order in Tzeltal and brings his whip down sharply on the horse's withers.

The Indians quicken their pace. We must reach Lomantán before the storm is upon us. But we're just over the crest of the hill when scattered drops begin to fall. At first it's only a light drizzle, and we're certain it won't last. But soon the rain gathers strength, and streams of water spill over the upturned brims of our hats and trickle between the folds of rubber capes that aren't large enough to cover us.

At last we see in the distance a village of simple, palm-roofed huts with lath-and-mud for walls. Scenting strangers, the thin, mangy dogs, drenched from the rain, come out to bark. Their commotion rouses the people who peer out their doors at us. They are Indians. Women with submissive expressions offer their breasts to the grasping mouths of newborn babies; pot-bellied, barefoot children; toothless old men with yellowish complexions.

My father goes ahead and reins in his horse in front of one of the huts. He talks with the man who seems to be the owner. But my father's arguments have little effect on the other's sullen composure. Father points to all of us, soaking wet from the rain. He explains that we need a fire to warm our food and a place to take shelter from the storm. From his pouch he takes some silver coins and offers them. The Indian has understood our plight but is reluctant to help. In spite of the scene before him, he continues to refuse with his sad, empty, expressionless face.

We have to go on ahead. We push through a mist that all but blinds us. The horses slide down the rain-softened slopes, or their hooves strike against the stones with a sharp, unpleasant sound. The Indians carefully make their way, measuring every step. . . .

We reach Chactajal at sunset. Gathered around the silk-cotton tree in the yard the Indians are waiting. They come near so that we can touch their foreheads with our fingers, and they give us little gifts: hens with their legs tied so they can't escape, fresh eggs, and small measures of corn and beans. Our task is to receive them graciously. Father gives the order for a large carafe of brandy and a bolt of cloth to be shared among them. Then we go to the chapel to give thanks for our safe arrival. They've decorated it as if it were a feast day, with garlands of ricepaper and with sedge strewn on the floor. On the altar the Virgin displays her silk dress embroidered with seed pearls. At her feet a large gourd filled with fruit emits a hundred mingled perfumes. Mother kneels and recites the mysteries of the rosary. The Indians respond in a single, anonymous voice.

After prayers we sit on the benches placed against the walls. One of the Indian women (one of the leaders, probably, judging by the respect the other women pay her), places in my mother's hands a gourd of *atole*.[3] Mother barely tastes it and passes it on to me. I do the same and hand it to the one beside me, and so on until we've all placed our lips on the same spot.

In one of the corners of the church the musicians are tuning their instruments—a drum and a reed flute. Meanwhile, the men, all lined up on the left, prepare to choose their partners for the dance. They clear their throats and snicker nervously. The women wait quietly in their places, with their hands folded in their laps. There they receive the red handkerchief thrown by the men, provided they want to accept the invitation to dance. Otherwise they casually let it drop, as if by accident, when they choose to refuse the offer.

The music—sad, sharp, harsh, like air passing over the bones of the dead —makes its sorrowful presence felt among us. The couples get up and stand quite still for a moment, facing one another at just the right distance. The women lower their eyelids, and their arms hang limp at their sides. The men lean forward, their hands behind their backs. They scarcely lift their feet from the ground as they dance for hours on end, shifting their weight from one foot to the other, calling insistently on an unknown being who does not respond.

The sedge loses its shine and its fragrance. The candles are all consumed. I lay my head, heavy with sleep, on my mother's shoulder. They carry me in their arms to the big house. Through my half-closed eyes I can see the flicker of the pine-flare burning in the yard and the palm leaves that cover the pillars of the veranda. And, in the shadows, the hostile gaze of those who refused to join in the festivities.

From my bed I can still hear—who knows how long—the monotonous rhythm of drum and flute, the crackle of the burning logs, the distant chirping of the crickets in the grass. And, now and then, the forlorn howl of a wild beast in the far away mountain.

"Who's there?"

I sit up trembling. In the darkness I can't make out the features of the shape that is standing before me. I think I can discern the form of an Indian woman, ageless, without a face.

"Nana!" I call out in a low voice.

The figure draws closer and sits on the edge of the bed. It does not touch me or breathe softly on my cheek or stroke my hair as Nana always does to lull me to sleep. But I hear these words in my ear:

"I'm here with you, my child. And I will come to you when you call, like the dove when the corn seeds are scattered. Sleep now. Dream that this whole, broad land is yours, that you are shearing oh-so-many peaceful sheep, that the harvest is full in the granaries. But beware that you do not wake up with your feet caught in the stocks and your hand nailed to the door. As if your dream had become an iniquity."

The Luck of Teodoro Méndez Acúbal

Walking along the streets of Jobel (with his eyes cast downward as custom dictates for those of his humble station), Teodoro Méndez Acúbal spotted a coin. All but lost in the dust, caked with mud, worn from years of use, it had been ignored by the white *caxlanes*. For the *caxlanes* walk with their heads held high. Moved by pride, they contemplate from afar the important matters that absorb them.

Teodoro stopped, more out of disbelief than greed. Kneeling as if to fasten one of his sandals, he waited until no one was looking to pick up what he had found. He hid it quickly in the folds of his sash.

He stood again, swaying, overcome by a kind of dizziness. Weak-kneed and dry-mouthed, his eyes blurred as he felt his heart pounding, pulsing between his eyebrows.

Staggering from side to side as if in a drunken stupor, Teodoro began to make his way down the street. From time to time the passersby had to push him aside to avoid bumping into him. But Teodoro's spirit was too troubled to be bothered by what was going on around him. The coin, hidden in his sash, had transformed him into another man—a stronger man than before, it is true. But also more fearful.

He stepped off the path that led to his village and sat down on a fallen log. Could this be all a dream? Pale with anxiety, Teodoro's hands felt his sash. Yes, there it was—firm and round—the precious coin. Teodoro unwrapped it, moistened it with his breath and saliva and rubbed it against his clothing. On the metal (it had to be silver, judging from its whitish color) the outline of a profile appeared. Majestic. And around the edge, letters, numbers, and signs. Calculating its weight, testing it with his teeth, listening to its ring, Teodoro was able—at last—to determine its value.

And so, with this stroke of fortune, he had become rich. Richer than the owner of great flocks of sheep or vast stretches of cornfields. He was as rich as . . . as a *caxlán*. And Teodoro was amazed that the color of his skin had not changed.

The images of the members of his family (his wife, his three children, his aging parents) struggled to invade Teodoro's reverie. But he dispelled them with an air of displeasure. He saw no reason to tell anyone about his discovery, much less share it. He worked to maintain his household. That's as it should be; it's the custom, an obligation. But as for this stroke of fortune, it was his. Exclusively his.

And so, when Teodoro arrived at his hut and sat down by the fire to eat, he did not speak. His own silence made him uncomfortable, as if being quiet were a way of mocking everyone else. To punish himself he allowed his feelings of loneliness to grow within him, along with his shame. Teodoro was a man set apart, stifled by his secret. Moreover, this anguish produced physical discomfort—a cramp in the pit of his stomach, a chill deep in the marrow of his bones. Why suffer all this, when with a word the pain would disappear? To keep himself from uttering it, Teodoro grasped his sash and felt the lump there, made by the metal.

During the sleepless night, Teodoro talked to himself: what shall I buy? Before now he had never wanted things. So convinced was he that they were beyond his reach that he passed them by without a thought, without the slightest curiosity. And now he wasn't about to consider necessities—a blanket, a machete, a hat. No. These are things to be bought with wages. But Méndez Acúbal had not earned this coin. It was his luck, an outright gift. It was given to him so he could play with it, so he could waste it, so he could have something impractical and beautiful.

Teodoro had no idea about prices. On his next trip to Jobel, he began to notice the dealings of buyers and sellers. Both appeared to be calm. The one feigning lack of interest, the other the desire to please, they spoke of pesos and centavos, of pounds and measures, of many other things that whirled about in Teodoro's head, making no sense at all.

Exhausted, Teodoro abandoned the struggle and took refuge in a delightful notion: with his silver coin he could buy anything he wanted.

Months went by before Teodoro made his irrevocable selection. It was a clay figurine, a small statue of the Virgin. It was also a real find, because the figure lay in the midst of a clutter of objects that decorated the window of a store. From that time on, Teodoro hovered around it like a lover. Hours and hours went by. And always he was there, standing like a sentinel beside the window.

Don Agustín Velasco, the merchant, watched him with his tiny squinting eyes (eyes of a hawk, his mother would say) from inside the store.

Even before Teodoro acquired the custom of appearing in front of his establishment, the Indian's features had attracted the attention of Don Agustín. No Ladino could help but notice a Chamula walking on the sidewalks (reserved for the *caxlanes*), and less so when he walked as slowly as if out for a stroll. It was unusual for this to happen, and Don Agustín had not even considered it possible. But he now had to admit that things might go further: an Indian was also capable of daring to stand before a window contemplating the display, not just with the assurance of one who can appreciate it, but with the bold insolence of one who comes to buy.

Don Agustín's thin, yellowish face grimaced in a gesture of scorn. For an Indian to go to Guadalupe Street to shop for candles for his saints, or whiskey for his festivals, or tools for his work is acceptable. The people who deal with them have neither illustrious lineage nor family names; they have no fortunes and therefore work at demeaning jobs. For an Indian to enter a pharmacy to ask for healing powders or liquid potions or miraculous ointments can be tolerated. After all, pharmacists belong to the middle-class families that wish to move upward and mingle with their betters, and that is why it's good for the Indians to humble them by frequenting their places of business.

But for an Indian to position himself so firmly in front of a jewelry store—no ordinary jewelry store at that, but the one belonging to Don Agustín Velasco, descendant of conquistadors, well received in the best circles, appreciated by his colleagues—was, at the very least, unfathomable. Unless . . .

A terrible thought began to gnaw at him. What if the boldness of this Chamula was based on the strength of his tribe? It wouldn't be the first time, the salesman admitted bitterly. Rumors . . . where had he heard rumors of revolt? Quickly Don Agustín tried to recall the places he had visited in the past few days: the Bishop's Palace, the Casino, the meeting at Doña Romelia Ochoa's house.

What foolishness! Don Agustín smiled, silently laughing at himself. How right Bishop Manuel Oropeza had been when he said that every sin has its punishment. And Don Agustín, who rigorously abstained from alcohol, tobacco, and women, was still a slave to one bad habit: gossip.

Slyly he made himself a part of conversations in doorways, in the market, even in the Cathedral. Don Agustín was the first to hear a rumor, to sniff out the scandals, and he longed for shared confidences, for secrets to guard and for intrigues to plot.

And at night, after supper (of thick chocolate provided by his anxious, worn-out mother), Don Agustín made a habit of attending a gathering of some sort. There they talked and entertained each other with stories. About love affairs, feuds over inheritances, sudden and unexplained fortunes, duels. For several nights the conversation had revolved around one topic: Indian uprisings. Everyone present had been witness, participant, victim, or victor in one or another. They recalled details of those they had seen. Terrible images that made Don Agustín tremble: fifteen thousand Chamulas ready for war, besieging Ciudad Real. Haciendas plundered, men killed, women (no, no, we must not think of these things), women . . . in the end, violated.

Victory always fell on the side of the *caxlanes* (anything else would have been inconceivable), but at such a price, such loss.

Is experience worth anything? Judging by the Indian standing at the window of his jewelry store, no. The inhabitants of Ciudad Real, caught up in their daily routines and interests, forgot the past, which should serve as a lesson to them, and went about their business as if no danger threatened. Don Agustín was horrified by such an irresponsible attitude. The security of his life was so fragile that all it took was the face of a Chamula, seen through a glass, to shatter it completely.

Don Agustín looked out again into the street hoping to find the Indian no longer present. But Méndez Acúbal remained there still, motionless and attentive.

The passersby walked near him without any sign of surprise or alarm. This consoling fact (and the familiar sounds that came from the back of the house) restored Don Agustín's sense of tranquility. He could no longer justify his fears. Events like the one at Cancuc, like Pedro Díaz Cuscat's siege of Jobel, and Pajarito's threats—those couldn't happen again. These were different times, more secure for decent people.

And besides, who was going to provide arms, who was going to lead the rebels? The Indian who was here, with his nose pressed against the window of the jewelry store, was alone. And if things got out of hand, no one was to blame but the townspeople themselves. No one was going to respect them if they themselves were not worthy of respect. Don Agustín disapproved of his fellow citizens' conduct, as if he had been betrayed by them.

They say that some—not many, thank God—even shake hands with the Indians. Indians—what a race of thieves!

The thought left a peculiarly painful taste in Don Agustín's mouth. Not only from a sense of propriety, as entrenched in him as in anyone else in his profession, but from a special circumstance.

Don Agustín did not have the courage to admit it, but what tormented him was the suspicion that he was himself insignificant. And to make matters worse, his mother confirmed his suspicions in many ways. Her attitude toward this, her only child (son of Saint Anne, she used to say), born when he was more a bother than a comfort, was one of Christian resignation. The "boy"— his mother and the servants continued to call him that in spite of the fact that Don Agustín was past forty—was very shy, cowardly, and passive. How many business deals had slipped through his fingers! And how many of those he did make resulted in nothing but failure! The Velasco fortune had dwindled considerably since Don Agustín took charge of things. And as for the prestige of the firm, it was maintained with great difficulty, and only because of the respect his late father, still mourned by mother and son, instilled in everyone.

But what could one expect from a wimp, an "overgrown child"? Don Agustín's mother shook her head sighing. And she kept on with her wheedling, her prudery, her condescending comments, for this was her way of expressing disdain.

Instinctively, the shopkeeper knew that he had before him the opportunity to prove his courage to others and himself. His zeal, his keen insight, would be evident to everyone. One simple word—thief—had given him the clue: the man with his nose pressed against the glass of his jewelry store was a thief. No doubt about it. Besides, the case was not uncommon. Don Agustín could think of countless anecdotes of robberies and even worse crimes attributed to the Indians.

Satisfied with his deductions, Don Agustín didn't settle for merely preparing a defense. His sense of racial, class, and professional solidarity obliged him to share his suspicions with the other merchants, and together they went to the police. The neighborhood was prepared, thanks to the diligence of Don Agustín.

But the person responsible for those precautions suddenly disappeared from sight. After a few weeks he appeared again in his customary spot and in the same posture: standing guard. Because Teodoro didn't dare go in. No Chamula had ever attempted such a bold act. If he were to risk being the first, surely they would throw him out into the street before his lice had a chance to escape into the establishment. But, if by remotest chance they didn't eject him, and if they allowed him to remain inside the store long enough to dicuss the matter, Teodoro wouldn't know how to express his desires. He could neither understand nor speak Spanish. And so, to unclog his ears, to loosen his tongue, he had been drinking Indian whiskey. The liquor had instilled in him a sense of power. His blood flowed, hot and fast, through his veins. The ease with which he moved his muscles dictated his actions. As if in a dream, he crossed the threshold of the jewelry store. But the cool dampness and the still, musty air inside brought him abruptly back to reality with a shock of terror. From a jewelry case the flashing eye of a diamond stared at him threateningly.

"May I help you, Chamula? What would you like?"

By repeating such pleasantries, Don Agustín sought to gain time. At the same time his hands searched for the gun he kept in the counter drawer. The Indian's silence frightened him more than any threat. He dared not raise his eyes until he had the gun in his hand.

The look he encountered paralyzed him. A gaze of surprise, of reproach. Why was the Indian staring at him like that? Don Agustín wasn't the one at fault. He was an honest man, he had never harmed anyone. And it appeared that he would be the first victim of these Indians who had suddenly set themselves up as judges! Here was his executioner, coming toward him with his fingers searching the folds of his sash, soon to draw forth who knows what instrument of death.

Don Agustín clutched the gun but could not fire. He cried out to the police for help.

When Teodoro tried to get away, he couldn't, because a crowd had gathered in the doorway of the store blocking his path. Shouts, gestures, angry faces. The police seized the Indian, questioned him, searched him. When the silver coin appeared in the folds of his sash, a shout of triumph arose from the crowd. Don Agustín excitedly held up the coin for all to see. The shouting exhilarated him.

"Thief, thief!"

Teodoro Méndez Acúbal was taken to jail. Since the charges against him were not unusual, no one was in a hurry to gather the facts of the case. His file grew yellow with age on the shelves of the police department.

The Cycle of Hunger

Alicia Mendoza awoke with pain in her neck and back. What a long trip! Endless hours on the bus. And the delay because they had to stop and change a tire. Throughout the entire trip the motor had rumbled on with great difficulty.

The view was not particularly interesting. Arid lands, desert plants. They passed Oaxaca after night had already fallen, yet Alicia struggled to see it through the window. She wanted to be able to write her friend Carmela that she had at least caught a glimpse of the most important city along the route. But she wasn't able to see much more than the hustle and bustle of the station.

Alicia tried to sleep the rest of the night. The seat was uncomfortable, and an overweight traveling companion was taking up some of her space. And yet she somehow managed to get settled and didn't wake up until the sun was already rising.

"How cold it is!" Alicia mumbled, warming her hands with her breath. The bus was slowly making its way through a dense fog. Through occasional breaks in the mist one could catch glimpses of mountain crests, pine branches.

Alicia was about to close her eyes once more when her neighbor warned, "You'd better be watching. We're about there."

She was smiling, wrapped in a woolen shawl, and seemed inclined to engage in conversation. But Alicia had other things on her mind. Could this town with its houses scattered all over the hillsides be Ciudad Real? She had not imagined it like this. When they told her she would be going to Chiapas, she had immediately envisioned a jungle, bungalows with fans, like in the movies, and cool drinks served over ice. But this chill, this fog, these humble cabins with shingled roofs. . . . What a pity! All the clothes she had bought would be totally useless.

"I'll have to spend my first paycheck on a coat," she thought, savoring the words: "my first paycheck." Alicia's godmother had died worrying because her goddaughter was not yet established in a career.

"What are you going to do when I'm not around," she would lament. "If only I could live to see you settled down. . . ."

As if it were that easy! She felt no calling to become a nun, nor did she have any prospects for marriage.

"Short and shapeless," a boy on the street once described Alicia. Young men didn't consider her attractive. They knew she was goodhearted, and they loved her like a sister. Little by little she became their confidante. She listened attentively, kept their secrets, gave them advice when they had troubles, and waited her turn, patiently, in those endless changings of partners that went on about her.

Her godmother just let her be. Poor Alicia! Orphaned and with a stepmother who hated her from the start and refused to take responsibility for her.

"But, for me—widowed and childless—Alicia has been a comfort. So gentle, so affectionate. She would make someone a fine wife. But men nowadays only notice the figure and the face."

In an attempt to compensate for all this, her godmother would buy her clothes and jewelry. That's the way she spent her savings. Until she became ill.

The diagnosis was clear, direct, and final: terminal cancer in its final stages. But Alicia had faith in miracles and trusted, until the end, that her godmother would be healed. "Is there anything that Saint Rita of Casia, advocate of the impossible, can't do? If I pray, she will be healed," she thought. And in the meantime she would cheerfully care for her ailing benefactor. During the agonizing months that followed, Alicia learned to give injections, look at wounds without getting nauseous, change dressings, identify the many medicine bottles, and know when each was needed.

Every cloud has a silver lining, they say. All of Alicia's experience was put to good use when she later took a job as a nurse.

Everything happened in a way that Alicia liked to call providential. Her friend Carmela, who had shared her grief and who was concerned about her future (besides being well-placed in society), had approached her about a position at the Indian Relief Mission in Chiapas.

"Does this have anything to do with the Church?" Alicia asked, with emotions too confused to analyze.

"Don't be silly!" was Carmela's retort. "You know very well that the Church is too poor. And in these heretical times!"

Alicia sighed as if a great load had been lifted from her shoulders. She had always feared winding up in a nun's habit on the icebergs of Alaska.

"Then it's operated by the government," Alicia deduced, somewhat apprehensively.

"Not that either. It's privately run—by kind-hearted people, people with means. You might say they are good stewards of God's bounty here on earth."

"Oh, yes, those elegant ladies who organize charity teas and fashion shows."

An angry look flashed in Carmela's eyes.

"Not them exactly, but their husbands. Businessmen, the kind that belong to clubs and get together every month at banquets. They're special people. You probably don't even know their names."

"Then they must be very demanding. And I don't even have a degree."

"That's no problem. If we use a bit of influence. . . . Anyway you have experience, and that's more important. Don't worry. The Mission is just getting started. They pay poorly; you'll have to be content with that, OK? Anyway, since they send people out in the middle of nowhere, they haven't the luxury of being very particular."

"Yes, of course. Do you know where they might send me?"

"To a clinic in Chiapas. Well, a kind of clinic. Besides, it's the only one there. The Mission has run into a lot of trouble. It seems that the building is very small. And there's just one doctor."

"His wife and I can keep each other company."

"I don't know if he's married," Carmela answered.

That doubt dispelled all of the objections Alicia was about to raise at the offer of the job. "That Chiapas is too far away and I won't have anyone to depend on; that the salary is a pittance. . . ." It doesn't matter, she told herself impatiently. There are other advantages. If someone had made her name them, she couldn't have. But in reality, she imagined herself living a great jungle adventure, with a handsome, unmarried, professional man, and in love. It could only lead to marriage. And Alicia, the doctor's wife, would spend her days hanging bright cotton curtains on the clinic windows and raising their children (many, all God sends our way) in the healthful country air.

Alicia spent the inheritance her godmother had left her, made herself clothes (low-neck dresses on account of the heat, but modest), and bought a bus ticket. Carmela went with her to the station to see her off.

"Is this your first time in Ciudad Real?" her fat traveling companion asked.

"Yes."

"Do you have any family or business in this area?"

"No. I've just come to work here."

"With the government?"

There was a certain suspicion in her voice.

"In the Indian Relief Mission."

"Oh."

The monosyllable was pronounced with a sarcastic tone that Alicia did not understand. She wanted to continue the conversation, but her neighbor suddenly became preoccupied counting her luggage and got off the bus without saying good-bye.

The fog had already lifted, but the day was overcast and disagreeable. Women crossed the street covered with huge black shawls.

"May I carry your bag, ma'am?"

It was a small ten-year-old boy speaking to Alicia. He was barefoot and had bristly hair. Many others had gathered around to try and take his job. He managed to scare them away with his fists and threats. Once he had won, he repeated his question. Alicia hesitated a moment, but had no choice but to accept.

"Is there a hotel that's not too expensive and fairly decent?"

The boy nodded affirmatively and they both began walking. The plaza, the arched arcades. The clock on the cathedral struck eight. At every step Alicia had to avoid running into Indians, who, carrying their heavy loads, moved quickly, panting as they went. Others were sitting on benches searching themselves for fleas or checking their supplies of provisions. As the little boy passed next to one of them, he gave the Indian a thump on the head. Alicia repressed a shout of alarm; she feared that this would result in a long, unpleasant scene. But the Indian did not even turn around to see who had hit him, and Alicia and the boy continued on their way.

"Why did you hit him?" she asked at last.

The boy scratched his head with a perplexed look on his face.

"Well, . . . just because."

Alicia's innate shyness and natural rectitude struggled within her. Trying to keep her words from seeming harsh or demanding, she urged the boy to refrain from such actions, since he might not always be able to get away with them so easily.

"Someone could hit you back . . . and they are older, stronger than you. . . ."

The boy smiled slyly.

"Am I an Indian for them to consider themselves my equals?"

They had arrived at the hotel. Its appearance was dismal. A big, old, rambling house with crude-looking numbers on the doors to the rooms.

A fat, placid woman hurried out to meet them. Alicia announced that her stay would be brief: only long enough to rest and freshen up a bit. If she were to show up as she was, she indicated by pointing at her wrinkled clothes, her tousled hair, she would make a very poor impression on her superiors.

"I came to work at the Indian Relief Mission," she went on, observing the effect that her words had on the proprietress.

The woman showed no sign of disapproval, but when it was time to pay the bill, its total had been altered upwards.

"You," she said to Alicia in answer to her protests, "come to Ciudad Real to make life more expensive. When the Indians are stirred up, they don't want to work on the farms anymore for what they were making; they're no longer willing to sell their wares at the former prices. We're the ones who suffer. It's only fair that you pay for the harm you cause us."

Alicia did not understand the reasoning behind this, but the tone of voice of her hostess had inhibited her. Hours later she mentioned the incident to the Mission director, a middle-aged man with no title, but according to some, with great administrative gifts.

"Well, now you've had your initiation, Alicia. As soon as they find out that you work with us, the shopkeepers and pharmacists, the shoe store owners, everyone, will charge you twice the price for these goods."

"But why? The Mission does them no harm."

"For those people there is nothing worse than someone who treats Indians like people; they have always considered them animals. Or when they become excessively humane, slaves."

"Is there no way to convince them that they're wrong?"

"I tried to do that at first. It was futile. Because here what's important is not reason but self-interest: the rancher who refuses to pay his Indian workers a living wage, the pharmacist who keeps supplying them with the poisonous concoctions they like to drink. . . . How can you argue? And now the battle lines have been drawn. You will soon discover through your own experiences just how underhanded the *coletos* . . ."

"The *coletos?*"

"That's what the whites of Ciudad Real are called. As I was saying, how many ways the *coletos* have of being hostile."

"And how can we defend ourselves?"

The director shrugged.

"That remains to be seen."

Alicia listened to his words in amazement. As of that moment her spirit, up to then motivated only by selfish concerns, became one with a body of people—the Mission—whose cause she now joined in its struggle to combat the *coletos* of Ciudad Real.

Alicia installed herself in the house that the Mission rented for its employees. She would be there only temporarily, since her final destination was the clinic in Oxchuc. But the roads were now impassable due to the rains. There was nothing to do but wait for drier days when the conditions would be favorable for leaving. In the meanwhile, Alicia had no particular task. She wandered through the offices, whose function she was never able to decipher. There were stacks of papers, files, typewriters, secretaries. A bell would ring peremptorily, followed by a small flutter with unpredictable consequences, and then the calm would settle in again. Yawns, impatient looks, furtive glances at the clock, a stimulating crossword puzzle, a secret piece of needlework. And at the end of the day, all the employees would smile, satisfied that they had fulfilled their responsibilities.

Alicia tried to be friendly, but her shy overtures were answered with the innuendos typical of the provincial *coletos*. They often wheedled her, hoping to elicit some personal tidbit they could later mock. But she ventured no further comments.

Feeling very disappointed, Alicia would go outside. In the hall (of a huge house that had been built with the marvelous idea of using it as a seminary or convent) were the Indians: all lined up, foul-smelling and identical, waiting to present their complaints. Problems with ranchers over land, outcries at the broken promises of middlemen who hired them to work. They talked animatedly among themselves. Alicia would smile and try to be sympathetic. But they never understood the feelings she tried to convey.

Finally she asked to see the director. Her inactivity was beginning to gnaw at her conscience, and she yearned for a meaningful assignment. The director smiled pleasantly.

"Don't worry. Your turn will come. We don't have a clinic here, so a nurse can't do much. What we need are lawyers."

"They say that there is a surplus of them in Ciudad Real."

"But none has wanted to help us. For them that would mean betraying their race, their people."

"And why not bring one from Mexico City?"

"Our resources are very limited. We can't afford to hire a professional with prestigious credentials. We have to take what we can get."

Alicia blushed violently.

"Mr. Director, I . . ."

"No, no, I didn't mean to offend you. I'm feeling my way along, myself. Of course, I have had some experience in business management. But what goes on here is so different. . . . Anyway, at least we mean well. And that is what the Association that gives us money expects of us."

The director stood to indicate that the meeting had ended.

"As for you, don't worry. Go on to your room and rest. You have to learn one thing from the Indians: that time means nothing."

It was raining incessantly. The clouds rolled in all morning and by noon a violent downpour was beating on the roof. In her room Alicia was brushing her clothes, trying to remove the green fungus that the humidity had caused to grow on them.

"When will I get out of here?"

The impossibility of leaving Ciudad Real distressed her greatly. One day it occurred to her that the doctor was also stranded at the clinic. And from that point on her anguish became more intense.

"Don't complain," Angelina, the director's secretary, told her. "It's better to be here than in Oxchuc."

"Is it such a sad little town?"

"It's not even a town. Two or three white people's houses and the rest Indians. Often there's nothing to eat."

"And what does the doctor do? Who takes care of him?"

"Salazar? I imagine that he's making deals with the devil. He spends months and months without coming to Ciudad Real. And when he comes he doesn't talk to anybody, doesn't even flirt with the girls. He gets very drunk and then spends the rest of his money on watches. They say he has quite a few."

Alicia decided that he had obviously suffered a broken heart. That must be why Dr. Salazar was so unsociable. The hypothesis encouraged her. After such an experience, a man really begins to appreciate a good-hearted woman. And a good heart was Alicia's specialty. She began to look at herself in the mirror less anxiously.

"And what is Dr. Salazar like? Handsome?"

Angelina thought for awhile. She had never considered him from that perspective.

"I don't know. . . . He's . . . he's distinguished."

For her, for all the single women of Ciudad Real, that was of utmost importance. A good catch. Someone to whom the well-to-do ladies, the landowners' and businessmen's daughters could aspire. Not a simple typist. Why should such an insignificant girl waste her time thinking seriously about him?

In June the rains began to let up.

"The roads aren't dry yet," the director said. "But we can't wait any longer. We'll send medicine and supplies to Oxchuc. This is a good time for you to go."

Alicia packed her suitcase, her heart pounding with joy. At last! With her own money she bought some canned goods. And for the greatest luxury, she bought some asparagus. She was certain the doctor would like them.

They left very early the following morning. The streets of Ciudad Real were almost deserted, but the few people who were out stopped, scandalized and amused at seeing the spectacle of "a woman riding a horse like a man." Their stares made Alicia uncomfortable, since it was her first time on a horse and she feared falling off at any moment.

The mule drivers and the cargo rode up front. Alicia brought up the rear. The horse understood immediately that its rider was a novice and took advantage of the fact to walk reluctantly, to run inopportunely, and to snort with the slightest provocation.

Alicia was numb from fear. The mule drivers secretly joked at her ineptness.

That was just the beginning. First, there were the mountains. Steep, rocky, with unlikely paths. The beasts slipped on the enormous slabs, stumbled on the loose sides. Or they got stuck in the mud up to their bellies, struggling desperately to move ahead.

Alicia looked at her watch. Only two hours had gone by. "How much longer would it be?" she asked. Each muleteer gave a different answer.

"There's not far to go, and it's completely flat."

"All rock, you mean," retorted another.

"It's more like four leagues."

"It's hopeless! We won't arrive before nightfall."

Meanwhile, the road kept unrolling, indifferent to all the predictions, varying its obstacles infinitely, offering new dangers at every turn.

"It's already getting dark," Alicia noted with surprise. She checked her watch once again. It was only three o'clock in the afternoon.

"It's the fog," explained the mule driver.

"Over this way it's always overcast. They say it's because of Saint Thomas, the patron saint of Oxchuc."

"And why?"

"He's a pain in the neck as a saint. Beginning with his not believing in Our Lord Jesus Christ. . . ."

"Son of a gun!"

"And so?"

"Well, here's how it was. One day Saint Thomas threw a huge stone up in the sky."

"Come on, now! You're not gonna tell me that the sky fell."

"And what did you want it to do? Our Lord Jesus Christ didn't want to pick it up. 'Let it teach that so-and-so a lesson,' he said. 'Let the one who knocked it down pick it up.' And ever since then Saint Thomas tries every day. But he'll never be able to do it! He lifts it a little, and later the sky gets too heavy and it falls on him again. That's what we call mist."

"Aren't you going to light the lamps?" Alicia asked.

"It's not necessary, ma'am; the horses know the way."

One of the mule drivers had been left with a big theological doubt.

"Hey, this Lord Jesus Christ you just mentioned, is that the same one that Saint Joseph holds?"

No one bothered to answer him. There was only mocking laughter.

The rest of the trip was made in the dark. To the known terrors Alicia added a thousand more imaginary ones: abysses, cliffs, snakes. All her muscles were tense. And then it began to rain.

It rained all night. The rain filtered through the rubber sleeves, the straw hats, until it penetrated the numbed bodies of the travelers. Alicia groaned silently with each move the horse made, at each turn in the road. Warm salty tears mixed with the water poured down her cheeks.

"Don't break down on me, ma'am, we're almost there!"

Alicia didn't believe these consolations. Since when had they been "almost there"? They would never get there or anywhere else. They were condemned to wander forever in the darkness.

First there was a yellowish, twinkling light far away. Then another, and then others, closer by. Oxchuc was in sight.

The prospect of arrival made the last few miles even more intolerable. Each step the horse took should have been its last, but was not. To endure the next one, Alicia had to call forth superhuman effort.

Dogs barking from hunger rather than anger came out of the huts, and one or two windows opened shyly. Alicia couldn't even turn her head to look because her neck was completely stiff. A few precarious adobe structures began appearing, and all of a sudden, unbelievably, they stood before the solid mass of a church and real town hall.

"There's the clinic," a mule driver pointed out.

As hard as she tried, Alicia couldn't make out a thing in the shadowy darkness. In a moment they were all stopping in front of a house, the same size and shape as all the others in town. Its only distinguishing features were the enormous letters that formed the initials of the Mission.

"Is this the clinic?" Alicia asked, a little faintheartedly.

"It has a fireplace!" announced one of the mule drivers.

"You need a key to get in. It's locked. The doctor must have gone out."

"We're all exhausted!"

"We'll have to go look for him."

"Let Sabás go; he knows where the doc goes to drink."

"Well, have him go at once!" Alicia urged.

She covered her mouth quickly, shocked by the peremptory tone of her voice. The mule drivers had not paid any attention to that; instead they were hurrying to obey her.

Alicia could not dismount without everyone helping her. She was paralyzed from the cold, and terror had caused her muscles to become immovably rigid. Almost dragging her, the mule drivers leaned her against the wall of the clinic.

There, at least, she was sheltered by the overhanging shingles. Huddled up, in order to escape the splashing of the rain and to retain the scarce heat of her body, Alicia fell asleep. She didn't wake up until the sun was high in the sky. Someone was shaking her and saying, "Here's the doctor, ma'am."

Alicia rubbed her face in dismay. How could she meet him looking like this, so battered and bedraggled? My God, she couldn't even stand up! She made an attempt that only resulted in a ridiculous fall. When she lifted her eyes, she saw a man watching her with mocking curiosity.

"So this is the nurse that came to save me from my plight!"

Alicia watched him anxiously. How old was this man? His unkempt beard and the lividity brought on by drinking and insomnia made it difficult to guess his age. His appearance was just as deplorable as her own.

Salazar must have read her thoughts, for he abruptly turned on his heels and walked away. He had the key to the clinic. From the back he appeared husky in his heavy sheepskin jacket.

Alicia caught up with him in the patio. The doctor was counting and checking the bundles that the mule drivers had brought. He grumbled.

"As usual, nothing we can use. Laboratory samples, leftover medicines that the rich no longer need. Sedatives, naturally. Not a vitamin or an antibiotic in the lot. Damn!"

Alicia breathed the slightest "oh!" It didn't occur to Salazar to beg her pardon. He looked at her severely.

"I hope that at least you know how to cook. I'm sick of those canned sardines."

"Yes, Doctor. I also brought some provisions," Alicia said excitedly, glad to be able to show off her abilities. "But I'm so dirty that I would like to take a bath first."

"A bath?" repeated Salazar as if she had just requested something absurd. Then he made a gesture of indifference. "If you want a bath, you'll have to go to the river. On foot. Anyway, I warn you that at this time of day the water is ice cold."

The mule drivers burst into laughter. Shaking from humiliation, Alicia resorted to wiping her face with a damp towel. She changed her muddied pants and put on a wrinkled dress. In this attire she made her way to the kitchen.

If her cooking ever pleased the doctor, she never knew it. Though she had very little to work with, she tried to create miracles by giving her meals variation and a pleasing appearance. But Salazar ate in silence, with an old newspaper open in front of him.

"What are you reading?" Alicia ventured.

"World news," Salazar condescended to reply, as if to a child or an imbecile.

Alicia cleared the table. In a copper-plated trough she washed the dishes, one by one, creating a deliberate and persistent noise.

"Whenever you want me to, Doctor, I am ready to help you in your office," Alicia announced a few days later.

Salazar raised his eyes, bothered by the interruption.

"Is there nothing to do at the house?"

Not that it bothered Alicia to do the work of a maid. Nevertheless, she felt certain that she was needed for more important tasks.

"I got a girl to come help me. Everything is in order. The only thing we haven't been able to do is to get the chimney to work. And with this cold . . ."

"The chimney is just a decoration. The draft doesn't work."

Alicia was not surprised. What else could one expect? She crossed her arms and awaited instructions. Salazar perceived her expectancy and in order to break it insisted, "So there's nothing left to be done. . . ."

"Only your room, and since you always lock it when you leave. . . ."

"I don't like anyone prying in my things."

Alicia had done just that, shamelessly and without results, since the beginning of her stay in Oxchuc. The only things she found were some scribbled papers, dirty clothes (some very ordinary women's clothing), and a fabulous box full of watches of all kinds.

"One day when I can watch you, I'll let you sweep my room. It's not possible right now. I'm going out."

"Some people are here to see you, Doctor."

"It's not time. The clinic is open from ten until two. We don't see anyone either before or after."

"Those poor people. They said they came from far away; they brought a sick man on a stretcher. I gave them a place in the hall."

"Well, you were wrong to do that! They're going to give us lice and who knows what else. Get them out of here at once."

"But, Doctor," protested Alicia, disconcerted, not understanding. . . .

"Well, if you don't understand, just do as I say. And I'm warning you, don't make assumptions on your own. I'm the only one responsible for this clinic."

"All right, Doctor. But are you going to have those who've been waiting leave just like that?"

The doctor struck the table with his newspaper.

"What do you want? For me to see the patient? What for? To take his pulse? The medicine they sent is already gone. I don't have any more to give him. Do you understand? Nothing."

"At least talk to them. They'll leave a lot happier if you would at least say a word to them."

"A word that those Indians don't understand; a word that would discredit me as well as the Mission, because it would be false. If I don't say anything, you think I'm unjust, which, by the way, doesn't bother me. If I talk, I lose their trust. And I need it. You don't know them. In spite of their humble ways, they don't come here for a favor. They come expecting miracles. They don't think of us as people just like them. They want to worship us like gods or destroy us like demons."

Alicia couldn't comprehend his reasoning. She was ignorant and uneducated without the benefit of years of experience like the doctor in Oxchuc.

"He's a man," she would tell herself. "He knows what he's doing. I have no right to criticize him."

But she could not dismiss the distaste she felt when she considered Salazar's conduct.

December came and brought with it an intolerable cold. Shivering, Alicia would huddle next to the useless fireplace. Sometimes the doctor left his newspaper and came over to talk. He would talk excitedly, making grand gestures. Alicia followed his stories with some difficulty. They were confusing, but they all dealt with the same thing: the student riots from which Salazar still had scars, since the police had broken them up violently. Later, to erase the bad memories, he would recall the soccer matches against the team from the University.

"Those of us from Polytechnic would fight with all our might. We'd try to beat them because they were the rich boys. We could blame them for all the evil in the world. How easy! But now. . . ."

"What about now?" Alicia asked, since the doctor did not seem inclined to continue.

"Now I know the poor."

He paused briefly. The expression on his face was one of cruel amusement.

"How stupid! For years I thought I was one of them. And I had to come to Chiapas, to Oxchuc, to find out that I hadn't the slightest idea of what poor was. And now I can say that I don't like what I've seen."

Alicia did not understand his method of judging. It never occurred to her to think of the poor as people to be accepted or rejected for the trouble they caused. She always associated them with charity, alms, compassion. His attitude irritated her.

"Why?"

"The rich exploit us, they abuse us. Right. But they leave us with the possibility, . . . or rather they make us defend ourselves. On the other hand, the poor beg, beg endlessly. They want bread, money, attention, sacrifice. They stand before us in their misery and make us feel guilty."

Salazar fell silent for a few moments. He seemed to be discovering something within himself.

"Could it be that I have become rich?"

Alicia smiled, "Forgive me, but it isn't noticeable."

"I mean, inside. As a student I lived on government grants. I slept wherever night fell. I ate whenever anyone invited me. I always judged, condemned the rest of the world. But now I have a place to live, not very comfortable, but secure. A job, not very sublime, but worthwhile. I earn a salary. I save. I buy myself things. You should see the watch collection I have."

"What are they good for here where time has no meaning?"

"That's precisely the key. When one can buy something completely useless, he's rich."

He began to pace the floor, taking great strides. Alicia watched him come and go and remembered that beside his watch collection was the pile of papers and the dirty clothes. "They belong to his lover," she was told by the girl that helped her with the housework. How disgusting!

"This complicates matters. Sometimes it's hard for me to distinguish between right and wrong. And here, you'll become aware, values aren't clear. Not clear at all. Whatever one does, it's always wrong."

Alicia was wrong a lot. Salazar never fulfilled her expectations. When, at last, she had reached the definite conclusion that the doctor was a man who had not the slightest concern for his chosen profession, she saw him come in, smiling from ear to ear.

"Good news! I just received a box of vaccine from Ciudad Real. Just let them throw those epidemics at us, we have something to fight them with now."

Alicia smiled half-heartedly. It was hard to regain her enthusiasm of earlier days.

"We'll set out with an interpreter and an assistant. You'll go with us; the presence of a woman lessens the suspicion. We'll go from village to village; there won't be a single child left vulnerable to whooping cough, diphtheria, or tetanus."

The committee left early the next morning. The paths were steep, and they advanced slowly through the rocks and quagmire. By noon they arrived at a village called Pawinal.

There were about thirty thatched huts scattered across the hillside. When the people of Pawinal saw strangers approaching, they ran to lock themselves inside.

"Why are they hiding?" Alicia asked.

"They're afraid. Their witch doctors have warned them not to receive us. And also the priest from Oxchuc."

"Why?"

"For different reasons. The witch doctors won't tolerate competition. We bring healing, too. Or, if you prefer, we also help them die."

"And the priest?"

"He doesn't know what to think. First, he said we were Protestants. Now he says we're Communists."

"That's slander!"

"Do you know what being a Communist is all about?"

"Well . . . no, not really."

"Neither does the priest. He says it in good faith. He assumes we represent a danger, and it's natural for him to want to protect his flock."

Months before, Alicia would have exclaimed, "That's incredible!" But since arriving in Chiapas, the limits of her credulity had become very elastic.

"What are we, Doctor?"

"They didn't tell you before you came? We're well-meaning people."

"Then we must tell them."

"Tell whom?"

"Everyone. To start with, tell these Indians."

"That's what the interpreter has been doing since we got here. He's going from house to house explaining that we're not out to gain anything for ourselves. That we're not going to exploit them, like the other whites do. That our desire is to help, to rid them of the threat of disease."

"But they're not even listening to him! Why do they run off or close the door in his face or cover their ears?"

"Because they don't understand what he's talking about. 'Well-meaning'! Those words probably don't even exist in their language. And as for the diseases we want to free them from, they are remote possibilities. However, with the shot we're going to cause them immediate illness: fever and pain. In whose name must they suffer? A germ whose existence they can't believe in because they've never seen it."

"So?"

"So, let's go. There's nothing we can do here."

Alicia was too tired to argue. They began the trip back. The interpreter, a white man from Oxchuc, was leading. He was whistling as if what happened actually made him happy. Behind came the doctor, lost in thought; the assistant, carrying the cargo; and Alicia, dejected.

At night, after having served the meal, Alicia came and sat down next to the doctor. She needed to talk to him, listen to his arguments, the justification for his actions that were always incomprehensible. She asked:

"Why do you work here?"

"I can give you two answers. One is idealistic: because everywhere one can help others. The other, cynical: because they pay me."

"Which is the real reason?"

"Both are, depending on what you choose to see. I studied very hard, made many sacrifices. I received very modest preparation studying to be a country doctor. I couldn't open an office even in the most meager town. My family was worried. I was their last hope! I had to hurry to prove to them that I wasn't a cheat. Then I heard about an association, a group of well-meaning people, as they like to call themselves, that was planning to send a doctor to a clinic in Chiapas. That was my chance."

"Were you here in Oxchuc from the beginning?"

"So far there's no other clinic."

"What did you expect to do?"

"Miracles. For others, a life of service. For me, the reward I needed: fame, fortune."

Alicia stood up, ashamed. She thought of her own motives: the salary too, the hope of getting married. How ridiculous! What right did she have to judge him?

"There's a great difference between what you hope for and what you get, right?"

"If we were honest, we'd resign."

"Why?"

"Because this is enough to drive anyone crazy. A clinic that has no medicine, a doctor that patients slam the door on, even a fireplace that doesn't work! It's a farce, Doctor, and I can't take it anymore! I want to get out of here!"

"Calm down, Sarah Bernhardt. It won't do you any good to get all excited. The best thing to do is to analyze the situation. It's not going well, I agree. But there must be a way to get to the root of the problem. If we find the error, we can work it out."

Alicia looked up, her eyes wide with hope. The doctor had a malevolent smile on his face.

"Until then we can enjoy all our advantages: a salary, a house, food. And time to spare. What do you enjoy doing? A lot of women like to knit; others read novels or just enjoy their leisure. Nowhere else will life be as easy as it is here."

"I know that. There would always be somebody watching me and making sure that I did as I was told, or they'd fire me."

"Good point. I don't owe you any explanations about my conduct since you're just a subordinate. However, I'm going to put your conscience at ease. Neither of us is defrauding anyone. They sent us here to work miracles: to multiply the medicines, to enlighten the minds of the ignorant. They sent us here to endure cold, solitude, and impatience. To share the misery of the Indians, or at least observe it, since we seem unable to do anything about it. It's enough for us to do this, in good conscience, to compensate for the salary they pay us. And by God, I swear that what they pay us isn't nearly enough!"

The light from the lamp was beginning to dim. Two colorless teardrops rolled down Alicia's cheeks. The doctor stood up.

"Meeting adjourned. If you want to take a sedative, there are some in the medicine chest."

Alicia remained seated awhile longer, in the growing darkness. Then, as mist filled the air, she walked across the patio. Lying on her cot she reflected on her ineffectiveness. Why hadn't she held her tongue? What was she trying to defend? Alicia's eyes, now dry, opened wide in the dark. She was afraid. She wanted desperately to run away, to be anywhere but there. In a clean world with good roads, where people were happy and healthy and could speak Spanish. That night she dreamed of her childhood home.

The expeditions were monotonous. Sometimes the doctor summoned Alicia. She assisted him, trembling with timidity, hurrying to comply—and often incorrectly!—with his orders. But under Salazar's gaze, her actions lost their meaning and became no more than absurd routine.

One night, very late, there was a knock at the door. Alicia awoke startled and, disregarding the doctor's direct orders, went to open the door.

Before her stood two Indians. In spite of their exhaustion and the awkwardness of their broken Spanish, Alicia was able to understand that they brought with them a woman, near death from a difficult labor. Alicia had them come in. The suffering on the woman's contorted face could be seen in the candlelight. They helped her onto Alicia's cot. Then she ran to the kitchen and put a pot of water on to boil.

"What's all the commotion?"

It was the doctor (still in his pajamas), speaking from the doorway.

Alicia walked toward him, imploringly.

"It's an emergency, Doctor. I couldn't leave them outside."

"Is someone hurt?"

"A woman in labor."

"How very strange! That's the witch doctor's job, or the midwife's. The doctor is only needed for accidents."

But while he was talking, Salazar didn't remain inactive. He was already in his room, getting dressed, and later in his office, disinfecting the instruments he would use. Alicia didn't have to urge him to hurry. The doctor watched over the patient all night with a diligence that Alicia could only attribute to their previous conversation. By morning a baby boy slept beside his mother, wrapped in makeshift diapers.

Salazar went to the kitchen to get a cup of coffee.

"That woman owes you her life, Doctor. If they don't make you the child's godfather, they ought to be ashamed."

"Who needs godchildren," Salazar protested. But Alicia's eyes caught a glimpse of secret satisfaction in the rough features.

"All I want to do is sleep. Don't wake me up unless it's an emergency."

"Don't worry, Doctor."

Alicia kept everyone quiet. The patient's husband and father-in-law walked on tiptoe through the clinic. The woman rested, holding her baby. Alicia lay down on the office couch. Several hours passed.

When Salazar awoke, he went to check on the patient and the baby. Everything was in order. So much so that his presence was no longer required there at the clinic. So he decided to go to a meeting at the municipal secretary's office. If anything came up, they could find him there.

"Meeting!" Alicia thought to herself. Cantina, you mean. Salazar always returned late from such gatherings. Oh, well. They'd just have to pray that calling him wouldn't be necessary.

Throughout the day Alicia prepared meals for the patient, who was weak from loss of blood. The Indian woman picked at her food so as not to appear rude. But she had no desire to eat, preferring only to rest. She fell asleep once more without realizing that night was falling. The next morning her baby's cries awakened her abruptly.

She tried to calm him by letting him nurse. The newborn sucked desperately for a few minutes and then began to cry again. He had not been able to get even a drop of milk. The mother looked around without understanding.

The baby's cry was at first choleric, strong and vigorous, but soon turned to plaintive whimpering. The Indian woman struggled to force milk from her breasts.

Her husband and father-in-law looked at one another knowingly, acknowledging the obvious truth. She had doubtless fallen victim to an evil spell. All women give birth easily, all women can nurse their babies. Why couldn't she? Was she guilty of some wrong and was this misfortune part of her punishment?

After a few moments of doubt and hesitation, Alicia sent the girl who helped her with the housework to find the doctor. Salazar arrived at the clinic furious and slightly drunk.

"What's going on here?" he asked as he entered.

"The woman doesn't have any milk," answered Alicia.

"Then give the kid some canned milk. In the medicine cabinet there's plenty, and bottles to put it in."

"But you took the key with you."

"All right, here it is. Get what you need. Check the prices and give the father the bill. But make sure you collect before you give them the milk or else you won't ever get paid."

Alicia was stunned. She didn't know that the Mission charged for its services. Salazar explained impatiently.

"It's a new rule I've made. Nothing out of the ordinary. Just a token charge. And enough of this. I have a right to rest, too, or don't I?"

Staggering, Salazar made his way toward his room while Alicia wrote up the bill. The cost of the can of milk and the feeding bottle was ten pesos.

"I don't have any money," said the younger Indian. The old man backed him up with a gesture of confirmation.

"It doesn't matter," Alicia started to say. "You can give it to me later."

What was important was to satisfy the baby's hunger. If they didn't pay her —one never knew what to expect from these Indians—she'd pay for it herself. It wouldn't break her.

Behind her she heard Salazar's voice.

"So there's no money, eh? I suspected as much, so I came back. There's no money. Well, go home and get some. Your son won't get a drop of anything until you come back."

Alicia turned to the doctor with eyes filled with disbelief. But Salazar, instead of repenting his decision, jerked the can of milk and the bottle from her hands.

"And as for you, Miss Nurse, I forbid you to give them anything without my authorization."

The doctor went to the medicine cabinet, put the things away, and locked it. Then he turned to the two Indians.

"I've known you a long time. You're can't fool me. Your last name is Kuleg; that means rich."

"But I have no money, sir."

"Check yourself well, unfold your belt. You, old man, maybe you have some money from Guatemala. You don't mind paying the witch doctor three or four hundred pesos, do you?"

The Indians lowered their heads and repeated the only words they knew: "We have no money."

Salazar shrugged his shoulders and without another word headed for his room. Alicia caught up with him just before he shut the door.

"We can't let that child die of starvation!"

"It's not our problem. There you have the new father, the grandfather. It's up to them to feed it."

"But they don't have any money."

"That's a lie! They do have money. I know that for a fact. The old man owns a corn field and some sheep. The young one could sign up to work on a farm on the coast and ask for money up front."

"And meanwhile, the child dies!"

The crying had ceased. Alicia grimaced with fear. Salazar smiled.

"Dying isn't as easy as you think. It's probably fallen asleep. And if not, what difference does it make? If that child dies today, it will be saved from thirty or forty years of suffering. To end up drunk or consumed by fever. Do you think it's really worth saving the child?"

"I don't care! You have no right to make that decision. Your duty . . ."

"What is my duty? Suppose I give Kuleg a can of milk. It would only last for a little while, three or four days at most. Then he'd be back for more. I know them, Alicia, they take advantage, like all Indians, like all poor people. And the clinic can barely support itself. It cannot give itself the luxury of raising children."

"Doctor, I beg you . . ."

Alicia would not listen to his arguments. She only wanted to run to the baby and put a bottle of warm milk in its mouth.

"What a fine example we would be! Today it's Kuleg who wants to take advantage of us. He has money. I am positive about that! Tomorrow it'll be someone else. And when we finish giving out all the medicine, then what? We won't have a cent to buy any more. But besides that, we will have lost a client. Because what is received without some sort of payment isn't valued. The witch doctor has more power than we do because he charges more!"

Alicia covered her ears. She moved away from Salazar quickly. In the patio she found the two Kulegs seated, smoking. She approached the younger man.

"I am going to give you the money, but don't tell anyone and go give it to the doctor. Hurry, before it's too late."

Alicia knelt down and was talking rapidly. She found a few coins that the two Indians contemplated without making the least effort of taking.

"The evil spirits are devouring my son."

This explanation, so simple, made any other action superfluous. Alicia turned to implore the older man. But he also looked at her with a stupefied gaze that the foreign words, the incoherent gestures, were unable to penetrate.

Alicia stood, defeated, and went to her room. The sick woman was sitting on the edge of the cot braiding her hair. Her face was still pale, but without traces of anxiety. The child was asleep sucking on its fist.

Alicia began talking hurriedly. She was shaking the Indian woman by the shoulders, as if to awaken her. She didn't protest. Though she quietly agreed to what Alicia asked, she understood little of the conversation. She was content to obey her husband.

Alicia left the room and went to the office. She tried for awhile to force the door of the medicine cabinet, but the lock would not budge. And she hadn't the strength to break it.

Exhausted from lack of sleep and from the events she witnessed so helplessly, Alicia sat on the ground under the eaves in the patio. Hours passed. Occasionally the hoarse crying of the child broke the silence. Then everything was quiet again.

At nightfall, the old man, his son, and the woman carrying a tiny corpse, left the clinic. Salazar had not yet awakened.

When he woke up, Alicia was packing her suitcases. Yawning, absorbed in thought, Salazar made no mention of what had happened.

"I've often told the Mission director that it isn't enough to put warm poultices on a wound. You've got to pull out the evil by the roots. Do you remember what we were talking about the other night? You must know what the real problem is. I have finally come to realize it. The real problem is educating the Indians. They must be taught that the doctor and the clinic are a necessity. They already know that necessities cost. If we just give them everything, they won't appreciate what they get. They're easily influenced by evil. I should know them. I've lived among them. Alone like a dog. Without anyone to talk to. And in fear. Fear of the revenge of the witch doctors, of the angry families because of those I couldn't save. How do they think I can save them? They bring them when they're almost dead. There's no gratitude. The credit always goes to someone else: the saint, the witch doctor. . . . But they're cowards, they only know how to kill through treachery. They never show their faces; they never look you in the eye. And with no one to talk to. The whites in Oxchuc are scheming, envious. You've got to watch out for them, too, because they'll do you in at any time. It takes guts to put up with all that. Before you came, I made my own meals because I was afraid they would poison me. There's no justice. A person prepares for a career, studies hard for years. There's no fun, no women, no nothing. And the family making sacrifices so you can get your diploma. Compensation will come, you think. And then they send you to rot in a place like this. Of course, I could leave whenever I wanted to. I'm a good doctor; you could never find a better one anywhere. It would be to my advantage. I need to see people, I need to find someone to tell, someone to explain to. Because I have discovered something, something very important. Good will isn't enough. What's essential is education, education. These Indians don't understand anything, and someone must begin teaching them. . . . Then you arrive with your fussiness and your nun-like manner and you find it easy to despise me because I get drunk once in a while and because you found out that I have a lover and because. . . ."

Alicia did not answer. Sobs were gripping her throat.

"Sometimes I wind all of my watches at once. It's nice to hear them run. They don't stop, nothing ever stops."

All of a sudden Salazar drew closer and took Alicia by the shoulders.

"What do you think is more important? The life of this little boy or the lives of all the others? Kuleg will tell them what happened. We taught them a lesson and what a lesson! Now the Indians will have learned that they can't play around with the Oxchuc Clinic. They'll start coming, sure they will! And with money up front. We'll be able to buy medicines, tons of medicine. . . ."

Salazar was illustrating his thoughts with dramatic gestures. Alicia moved away from him. When she'd finished packing her clothes, she closed the suitcase. Outside the rain was falling.

From Oficio de tinieblas *(Tenebrae Service)*

CHAPTER 1

Saint John the Protector, the one who was present when the worlds first appeared, the one who gave approval for the century to begin, one of the pillars that holds firm that which is firm, Saint John the Protector looked down one day to contemplate the world of men.

His eyes went from the sea where the fishes play to the mountain where the snow sleeps. They passed over the plain where the wind mounts its fury, over the beaches of shimmering sand, over the forests made for the animals' cautious roaming, over the valleys.

The gaze of Saint John the Protector fell upon the valley that is called Chamula. He was pleased with the softness of the hills as they came breathlessly from afar to seek repose here. He was pleased with the nearness of the sky, and with the morning fog. And it was then that the spirit of Saint John was moved with the desire to be revered in this place. And so that there would be no lack of material for the building of the church and so that the church would be white, Saint John turned all the white sheep of all the flocks grazing there into stones.

The promontory, silent and motionless, remained there as a sign of good will. But the tribes that populated the valley of Chamula, the Tzotzil bat-men, did not know how to interpret the sign. Not even the elders, nor the men of the council, were able to offer a valid opinion. All was confused muttering, downcast eyes, arms failing in fearful gesturing. Because of this, other men had to come later. And these men came as if from another world. The sun was in their faces and they spoke in a haughty tongue, a tongue which strikes fear in the heart of those who hear it. A language, not like the Tzotzil, which is spoken also in dreams, but instead an iron instrument of lordship, a weapon of conquest, the sharp scourge of the law. Because how, if not in Castilian, are orders given and sentences declared? And how is it possible to punish and reward if not in Castilian?

But not even the new arrivals understood exactly the enigma of the petrified sheep. They only understood the command that gives orders to work. And they with their heads, and the Indians with their hands, began the construction of a temple. By day they dug a ditch for cement, but by night the ditch became level. By day they raised the wall, and by night the wall fell. Saint John the Protector had to come in person, pushing the rocks himself, one by one, making them roll down the slopes until they were all gathered in the place where they were to remain. Only then did the efforts of the men achieve their reward.

The building is white, just as Saint John the Protector wanted it to be. And since that time the consecrated air above the altar resounds with the prayers and the songs of the white *caxlán,* the laments and supplications of the Indian. The wax burns in total immolation of itself; the incense exhales its fervent soul; the cypress boughs refresh and perfume the air. And from the most eminent niche of the main altar the image of Saint John the Protector (finely silhouetted in polychromed wood) keeps watch over the other images: Saint Margaret with her tiny feet, the giver of gifts; Saint Augustine, robust and serene; Saint Geronimo, with the tiger in his entrails, secret protector of witches; Our Lady of Sorrows, with a stormcloud reddening her horizon; the enormous cross of Good Friday, demanding its annual victim, poised as if on the brink of crashing down like a catastrophe. Hostile powers that had to be restrained so as not to unleash their forces. Anonymous virgins, mutilated apostles, unwieldy angels tumbled in turn from altar to bier and to the floor, where they then fell prostrate. Matter without virtue, which piety forgets and oblivion disdains. Unhearing ear, indifferent breast, closed hand.

And that is the way things were said to have happened from the beginning. It is true. There are testimonies. They can be read on the arches of the door at the entrance to the temple, from whence the sun bids its farewells.

This place is the center. The three communities of Chamula surround it: the seat of government, the religious and political center, and the ceremonial city.

To Chamula the Indian dignitaries come from the most remote places in the highlands of Chiapas, where Tzotzil is spoken. Here they receive their assignments.

The office with the greatest responsibility is that of president and, next to it, that of scribe. They are assisted by mayors, aldermen, elders, governors, and alms-keepers. There are stewards who are entrusted with the care of the saintly images and ensigns to organize the sacred festivals. These "passions" are set during Carnival week.

The assignments last twelve months, and the officers, transitory inhabitants of Chamula, occupy the huts scattered across the hills and plains, supporting themselves by working the land, raising farm animals, and tending herds of sheep.

Upon the conclusion of the term, the representatives, bestowed with dignity and honor, return to their villages. They then enjoy the status of "former authorities." They spent many hours in deliberation with their president, and the deliberations were reported in the written record, on "paper that speaks," by the scribe. They settled matters of boundaries, abolished rivalries, established justice, tied and untied marriage unions. And, most importantly, they were privileged to serve the divine. It was entrusted to their care for vigilant protection and reverence. And thus the chosen ones, the flower of the race, are not permitted to enter the divine presence during the day with work-feet but rather with prayer-feet. Before beginning any task, before pronouncing any word, the man who serves as an example to the others must prostrate himself before his father, the sun.

The sun rises late in Chamula. The rooster crows to disperse the fog. Slowly the men stretch. Slowly the women stoop and blow the ashes to uncover the faces of the coals. Around the hut the wind roams. And under the thatched roof and between the four walls made of mud, the cold air is the guest of honor.

Pedro González Winikton separated his hands, which meditation had joined together, and let them fall at his sides. He was an Indian of great stature and firm muscles. Despite his youth (that premature, severe youth typical of his race) others came to him as if he were an elder brother. The accuracy of his decisions, the zeal of his commands, the purity of his customs, gave him a certain status among the respected people, and only in the execution of his duties did his heart sing within him. And so, when it fell his lot to accept the investiture of judge, and when he took his vows before the cross in the atrium of the Church of Saint John, he was happy. His wife, Catalina Díaz Puiljá, wove a garment out of thick, black wool that covered him fully to the knee. So that he would be highly regarded in the assembly.

Therefore, as of December 31 of that year, Pedro González Winikton and Catalina Díaz Puiljá established themselves in Chamula. They were given a hut in which to live and a plot of ground to farm. The maize field was there, already green, promising a bountiful harvest. What more could Pedro desire if he already had material abundance, prestige among his equals, the devotion of his wife? Unable to express his deep satisfaction, the smile on his face endured for an instant. His countenance again became rigid. Winikton thought of himself as a hollow stalk, the stubble that is burned after the harvest. He also compared himself to a weed. Because he had no children.

Catalina Díaz Puiljá, barely twenty years old but already withered and tired, was given to Pedro by her parents when she was still a child. The early days were happy. The lack of issue was viewed as normal. But later, when the companions with whom Catalina spun yarn and gathered water and wood began to walk a little more heavily (because they carried both themselves and the one to come), when their eyes became peaceful and their wombs began to swell like a full granary, then Catalina felt her fruitless hips, cursed the lightness of her step, and, suddenly turning to look behind her, found that she left no footprints. And she felt anguish thinking that her name would pass from the memory of her village in the same way. And from then on she could not rest.

She consulted with the elders, thrust her pulse to the ears of the soothsayers. They investigated the circulation of her blood, gathered facts, consulted among themselves. Where did your road turn, Catalina? Where did you go astray? Where was your spirit made afraid? Catalina sweated, overcome by the vapor of the miraculous herbs. She did not know how to respond. And her moon did not turn white like those of women who can conceive, but it was dyed red like the moon of single women and widows. Like the moon of the women of pleasure.

Then the pilgrimage began. She went to the *custitaleros,* the wandering people who were always informed of the latest news from afar. And in the deepest recesses of their minds they kept the names of the places she needed to visit. In Cancuc there was an old woman who served as a spell-caster or as a sorceress, depending on how she was needed. In Biqu'it Bautista a witch probed the depths of the night to interpret its designs. In Tenejapa lived a witch doctor of excellent reputation. Catalina sought advice from them all, bearing her humble gifts: the first tender ears of corn, large carafes of liquor, a baby lamb.

And so, for Catalina the light of hope began to grow dim, and she shut herself away in a somber world ruled by arbitrary forces. And she learned to appease these forces when they were adverse, to encourage them when they were propitious, to manipulate their portent. She repeated brutalizing litanies. Deliriously she ran through flames of fire without being harmed. She had now become one of those who dared to look mystery straight in the eye. An *ilol* in whose lap rest many spells. Anyone she looked upon with a frown would tremble; anyone she smiled upon felt relief. But Catalina's womb was still closed. Closed as tight as a nut.

Out of the corner of her eye, as she knelt before the stone to grind the day's ration of meal, Catalina studied the silhouette of her husband. When would he repudiate her? How long would he endure the insult of her sterility? Marriages like theirs were customarily thought invalid. One word from Winikton would be enough to send her back to her family's hut in Tzajal-hemel. She would no longer find her father there, for he had died years before. She would no longer find her mother there, as she too had passed on. The only one left was her brother Lorenzo, known to all as "el inocente" because of his simplemindedness and the empty laugh that distorted his face.

Catalina stood up and put the ball of dough in her husband's knapsack. What kept him with her? Fear? Love? Winikton's face hid his secret well. Without a gesture of farewell, the man left the hut. The door closed behind him.

An irrevocable decision froze Catalina's countenance. She would never allow a separation; she refused to be left alone; she would not be publicly humiliated!

Her movements became more lively, as if she were fighting an adversary then and there. She moved about her hut, guiding herself more by touch than by sight, since the light penetrated only through the holes in the wall, and the room was darkened, filled with smoke. Even more than touch, habit directed her movements, keeping her from knocking over the objects that were piled up haphazardly in the cramped space. Pots of clay, chipped and broken, the grinding stone—too new, not yet dominated by the strength and ability of the grinder—tree trunks instead of chairs, ancient chests with broken locks. And, reclined against the fragile sides of the hut, innumerable crosses—a wooden one whose towering height seemed to uphold the walls, the others of intertwined palm leaves, small and butterfly-like. Hanging from the central cross were the initials of Pedro González Winikton, Judge. And scattered on the floor were the tools of trade of Catalina Díaz Puiljá, Weaver.

The murmur of activity coming from the other huts, increasingly distinct and pressing, made Catalina shake her head as if to scare away a bad dream that tormented her. She hurried to complete her preparations. In a net she carefully placed the eggs gathered from a nest the night before, wrapped in leaves to avoid their breaking. When the net was full, Catalina carried it on her back. The leather band that dug into her forehead gave the impression of a deep scar.

A group of women had gathered around the hut in silence to await Catalina's appearance. One by one they paraded in front of her, bowing with respect. They did not raise their heads until Catalina touched them with her fleeting fingers and mechanically recited the salutation of courtesy.

When this ceremony was complete, they went on their way. Even though they all knew the road, not one dared take a step without following the *ilol*. It was evident from their expectant, solicitous overtures that these women considered her a superior. Not out of respect for her husband's position, since all were wives of public officials and some of higher rank than Winikton, but because of the fame that transformed Catalina in the eyes of these unfortunate, fearful souls, so eager to ingratiate themselves with the supernatural.

Catalina allowed the veneration with the calm certainty of one receiving her due. The submission of the others made her neither uncomfortable nor vain. Her conduct was one of tactful but grudging response to the tribute paid her. Her reply was an approving smile, an understanding look, an opportune counsel, a fortuitous observation. And yet she always went armed with the threatening possibility of causing harm, though she herself was careful to keep her power in check. She had already seen how often the mighty had fallen.

And so, Catalina marched at the head of the procession of Tzotzil women, all uniformly dressed in thick, dark garments. All bent under the weight of their burdens (wares to sell, sleeping babies). All on their way to Ciudad Real.

The path, made by constant travel, wound around the hillsides. Loose, ochre earth, the kind that is easily swept away by the wind. Hostile vegetation. Weeds, twisted thorns. And all along the way, shrubs, bushes, peach trees dressed in their finery, smiling and glowing with happiness.

The distance between Saint John Chamula and Ciudad Real (or Jobel in the Indian language) is long. But these women could travel it without growing tired, without conversation. Attentive to where they placed their feet and to the labor of their hands, which produced wheels of woven threads that grew longer with each step.

The massive chain of mountains comes to rest in an extensive valley. Here and there, scattered as if allowed to fall carelessly, the houses appear. Tile-roofed buildings, dwellings of the Ladinos who tend their flocks and gardens, they offer precarious refuge from the weather. At times, with the insolence of its isolation, a hacienda comes into view. Strong and solid, its sinister appearance is more like that of a fortress than a dwelling for the idle rich.

Outlying areas, suburbs. From there one can see the towers of the churches, reflecting the light in the moisture-laden air.

Catalina Díaz Puiljá stopped and crossed herself. Her followers imitated her. And then, amid hurried whispers and skillful maneuverings, they redistributed the merchandise they were carrying. Some women took all they could carry. The others only pretended to bend under their heavy loads. These went on ahead.

Quietly, like those who neither see nor hear, who expect no sudden disturbance, the Tzotzil women went on their way.

When they turned the first corner, it happened—no less fearful and repulsive by being expected or habitual. Five Ladino women from the lower class, barefoot and poorly dressed, attacked Catalina and her companions. Without a word of threat or insult, without explaining why, the Ladino women tried to snatch the nets of eggs, the clay pots, the cloth, from the hands of the Indian women, who defended themselves with brave and silent furor. But in the midst of the fight, both sides took care not to damage or break the disputed objects.

Taking advantage of the confusion of the first few moments, some of the Indian women were able to escape and ran into the center of Ciudad Real.

Meanwhile those who remained behind opened their injured hands and surrendered their belongings to the attackers, who triumphantly took possession of the bounty. And to give their violence the appearance of legitimacy, they hurled a fistful of copper coins at the enemy, who knelt, weeping, and gathered them from the dust.

Cooking Lesson

The kitchen is sparkling white. What a shame to have to disturb it by cooking dinner. One should just sit and contemplate it, discover it, close one's eyes and meditate on it. If one stops to consider, this neatness, this beauty is nothing like the glaring brightness that produces chills in a hospital. Or is it the aura of disinfectant, the soft, hurried steps of eager attendants, the lingering presence of illness and death? But what does that matter to me? My place is here. Since the beginning of time, it has been here. Like the German proverb says, woman is synonymous to "Küche, Kinder, Kirche." I was lost in classrooms, streets, offices, cafés—wasting myself on tasks I must now forget in order to take on others. For example, selecting a menu. How could I manage such an unlikely undertaking without the help of tradition and historical perspective?

On a special shelf, all in a line and easy to reach, are my protective spirits —those wonderful equilibrists that use the pages of cookbooks to reconcile the most outrageous contradictions: trimness and gluttony, extravagance and economy, celerity and succulence, and . . .

What would you suggest for today's meal, experienced homemaker, inspiration of mothers both absent and present, voice of tradition, secret whisperings in supermarkets? I open a cookbook at random, and I read: "Don Quijote's Supper." Very literary but very unsatisfactory. Because Don Quijote was known as an absent-minded dreamer, not a gourmet. Although a more careful analysis of the text reveals that . . . etc., etc., etc. Ugh. More ink has been spilled on that subject than water under a bridge. "Fowl Face Up." Esoteric. What kind of face? How can anything cooked have a face? If it does, it couldn't be very appetizing. "Veal à la Rumanian." I wonder who the Rumanian is? If I knew what tarragon and scallions were, I wouldn't have to consult this book because I would be all-knowing. If you had the slightest concept of reality, you or one of your colleagues should take the time to write a dictionary of technical terms, include some preparatory remarks, think up an introductory lesson to make your very difficult culinary art accessible to the average person. But they presume that we are all into matters of garlic, and so they are satisfied with simply launching forth. I, for one, solemnly declare that I am not, and have never been, interested in this sort of thing. I have never understood it at all. You can observe the symptoms. I stand there like an imbecile, in an impeccable and sterile kitchen, in an apron that I wear as a transitory symbol of efficiency.

I open the meat compartment of the refrigerator and extract an unrecognizable package covered with crystals of ice. I plunge it into hot water, and the label, without which I would never have been able to identify its contents, comes into view: a pot roast. Magnificent. A simple, healthful meal. Since it requires neither scientific expertise nor intellectual challenge, it doesn't appeal to me.

It is not only excessive logic that spoils my appetite. It is also the way the meat looks, rigid from the cold and the color it has taken on now that I have unwrapped it. As red as if it were about to start bleeding any minute.

My husband and I had backs about the same color after our orgy of sunbathing on the beaches of Acapulco. He could afford the luxury of "playing his role" and lying face down to protect his throbbing skin. But I, the self-sacrificing little Mexican wife, born like a dove for her nest, smiled serenely like Cuauhtemoc in his torment and said with him, "this is but a bed of roses." Lying on my back, I had to support not only my own weight but my husband's as well. The classic position for lovemaking. And I moaned from pain and pleasure. The classic moan. Ah, myths, myths.

The best part (at least for the sake of my sunburn) was when he fell asleep. At the touch of my fingertips—insensitive from their prolonged contact with typewriter keys—the nylon of my bridal nightgown failed in its fraudulent attempt to simulate lace. In the dark of the night, I stroked the buttons and those other decorations that make the wearer appear very feminine. The perfect whiteness of my clothing, deliberate, reiterative, shamelessly symbolic, was suddenly gone. Perhaps for an instant it achieved its purpose in the light and under the gaze of those eyes now overcome with exhaustion.

Eyelids that close and leave me once again alone. An enormous expanse of sand with no escape but the ocean, whose movement suggests paralysis, with no invitations but a cliff for suicide.

But it's all a lie. I am not the sleep that dreams and dreams and dreams again. I am not the reflection of an image in the glass. A hardened conscience or all possible consciences do not destroy me. I continue to live a dense, viscous, turbid life, even though the one by my side and the one far away may ignore me, forget me, put me off, abandon me, stop loving me.

I am also a conscience which can close itself off, forsake another, and expose him to annihilation. I . . . The meat, under its spray of salt, has quieted its scandalous redness and is now more tolerable, more familiar. It is the piece that I have seen a thousand times, without realizing it, when I peeked in quickly to tell the cook that . . .

We were not born together. Our meeting was strictly by chance. Happy? It's still too soon to tell. We met at an exposition, at a conference, at a movie. We ran into each other in the elevator. He gave me his seat on the bus. A park ranger interrupted our perplexed and, until then, mutual contemplation of a giraffe because it was time to close the zoo. One of us, he or I, it doesn't matter, asked the foolish but necessary question: "Do you work or study?" Similar interests and good intentions, indication of the "seriousness" of our purposes. A year ago I had no idea of his existence and now I am lying next to him with our thighs interwoven, wet from sweat and semen. I could get up without waking him, go to the shower barefoot. To purify myself? I don't feel shame. I prefer to believe that what ties me to him is something as easy to wash away as a secretion, and not as terrible as a sacrament.

So I remain motionless, breathing rhythmically to feign repose, polishing my insomnia, the only jewel of maidenhood that I can and want to keep as long as I live.

Under the light deluge of pepper, the meat has turned grey. I rub away this symbol of age as I pierce its surface to saturate its depths with the spice. Because I have lost my former name and am not yet accustomed to the new one (which is not yet fully mine), the bellman's call falls on unhearing ears. I am overcome with that vague, sick feeling which is a prelude to recognition. Who is this person that doesn't answer his call? It could be something urgent, serious, definite, a matter of life or death. The one who is calling despairs, disappears without a trace, without a message, precluding any possibility of a new encounter. Is it anxiety that grips my heart? No, it is his hand pressing on my shoulder. And his lips that smile benevolently, more like those of a magician than a master.

And so as we walk toward the bar (my shoulder is burning, my skin is peeling), I accept the fact that my contact or collision with him has caused a deep change in me: once I didn't know and now I know; once I didn't feel and now I feel; once I was not and now I am.

I'll have to leave it at that. Until it reaches room temperature, until it absorbs all the spices I've covered it with. I have a feeling that I haven't calculated correctly and have bought a piece too big for just the two of us. I, out of laziness, am not a meat-eater. He, out of a sense of the aesthetic, tries to keep in shape. Most of it will be left over! Yes, I know I shouldn't worry. One of the spirits that hovers about me will come to my rescue and explain to me how to make good use of the scraps. It is a false step at best. One does not begin married life in such a sordid way. And I fear, too, that one should not begin it with a meal as uninteresting as a pot roast.

Thank you, I murmur, as I wipe my lips with the corner of a napkin. Thank you for that diaphanous drink, for the submerged olive. Thank you for having freed me from the cage of one sterile routine only to enclose me in another that, according to all the plans and possibilities, should be a fruitful one. Thank you for giving me the opportunity to wear a long flowing dress, for helping me move down the aisle of the church, exalted by the organ music. Thank you for . . .

How long before it's done? Well, it shouldn't matter that much, since it has to be put in the oven at the last minute. It doesn't take long, the cookbooks say. How long is "not long?" Fifteen minutes? Ten? Five? Naturally, the text doesn't specify. It supposes that because of my sex, I possess an intuition I do not possess, a sense I was born without, that would allow me to know the precise moment when the meat is ready.

And you? Have you nothing to thank me for? You have made your point solemnly and pedantically and precisely, in words meant to flatter rather than offend: my virginity. When you discovered it, I felt like the last dinosaur on a planet where the species was extinct. I attempted to justify myself, to explain that if I came to you intact, it was not out of virtue or pride or homeliness, but rather because of my own particular style. I am not baroque. A small imperfection in a pearl is unbearable to me. My only alternative is neoclassicism and its rigidity is incompatible with the spontaneity of making love. I lack the flexibility of a rower, a tennis player, or a dancer. I do not participate in any sport. I perform a ritual, and the act of submission petrifies me like a statue.

Do you long for me to be spontaneous, do you expect it, do you need it? Or is this sacred rite that you interpret as my natural passivity enough for you? And if it happens that you are inconstant, it will ease your mind to know that I will not interfere with your adventures. Thanks to my temperament, you won't have to fuss over me, or shackle me with children, or smother me with syrupy resignation. I will stay just as I am. Still and quiet. When your body covers mine, it is like a gravestone, full of inscriptions, and other people's names, and memorable dates. You moan inarticulately and I want to whisper my name in your ear so that you will remember who it is that you possess.

It is I. But who am I? Your wife, of course. And that title is enough to distinguish me from all the memories of the past, and all the plans for the future. I bear the mark of ownership, but still you look at me with distrust. I am not weaving a net to catch you. I am not a praying mantis. I am grateful that you believe such a hypothesis. But it is false.

This meat is tough and has a consistency uncharacteristic of beef. It must be mammoth. Like those that have been preserved since prehistoric times in the icecaps of Siberia and people thaw them and season them for food. In the boring documentary they showed at the Embassy, so full of superfluous details, they made not the slightest mention of how long it took to make the meat edible. Years, months. And here I am with only . . .

Is it a lark? Is it a nightingale? No, our timetable won't be governed by those winged creatures that warned Romeo and Juliet of the dawn, but rather by the thunderous precision of an alarm clock. And you will not descend at daybreak by my braids but rather by the stairway of trivial complaints: a button missing from your coat, burned bread, cold coffee.

I will stew silently in my bitterness. I have all the responsibilities and duties of a servant. I am to keep the house spotless, the clothes pressed, the meals on schedule. But I am not paid a salary, I am not given a day off each week, I cannot change masters. I must, on the other hand, contribute to the maintenance of the household and effectively execute the tasks the boss demands, the co-workers argue about, and the subordinates hate. In my leisure I become a social butterfly, who gives luncheons and dinner parties for her husband's friends, attends meetings, supports the opera, watches her weight, renews her wardrobe, takes care of her skin, keeps herself attractive, stays up-to-date on all the gossip, works late and rises early, runs the monthly risk of motherhood, believes in evening executive sessions, in business trips, and in the unexpected arrival of clients, suffers olfactory hallucinations when she perceives the scent of French perfumes (different from the ones she uses) on her husband's shirts and handkerchiefs, refuses to spend those lonely nights pondering the whys and wherefores of all the bother, fixes herself a stiff drink, and goes to bed with a good who-done-it, like a fragile convalescent.

Wouldn't it be a good idea to turn on the stove? A very low flame to preheat the roasting pan "which has been greased so the meat doesn't stick." Even I would have thought of that. It wasn't necessary to waste the pages of a cookbook with such a trivial piece of advice.

And yes, I am very clumsy. Now it's called clumsiness; before it was called innocence and you loved it. But I have never liked it. When I was single I would hide away and read things. Sweating from emotion and shame. I never became informed about any of it. My temples throbbed, my eyes became clouded, my muscles contracted in a spasm of nausea.

The grease is beginning to boil. I put in too much—how wasteful—and now it is sizzling and popping out to burn me. That's how I'm going to burn in those bottomless pits of *mea culpa, mea culpa, mea maxima culpa.* But, my dear, you're not the only one. All your friends from school do the same thing or worse. They confess to the priest, do their penance, receive forgiveness, and return to their same old ways. All of them. If I were still hanging around with them, they'd be asking me all kinds of questions now. The married ones to assure themselves, the single ones to find out just how far they can venture. I couldn't disappoint them. I'd invent clever maneuvers, sublime languishings, raptures like those in the *Arabian Nights,* statistics. Even Casanova wouldn't recognize himself if he could hear me go on!

I let the meat fall into the roaster and instinctively back up against the wall. What a racket! But now it's stopped. The meat just lies there quietly, faithful to its corpse-like condition. I still think it's too big.

And it's not that you've let me down. It's true that I wasn't expecting anything in particular. Little by little we will open up to one another, revealing our secrets, our little quirks, learning how to make each other happy. And one day you and I will be a pair of perfect lovers and then, in the midst of an embrace, we will simply vanish and the words "The End" will appear on the screen.

What's happening? The meat is shrinking. No, no, it's not my imagination; I'm not making it up. A perfect outline of its original size can be seen right there on the pan. It was a little larger. Well, OK! I hope it shrinks to fit our appetites.

In the next movie I would like to have another role. A white witch in a village of savages? No, today I'm in no mood for heroism or danger. Maybe a celebrity (a fashion designer or something like that), independent and wealthy, living alone in an apartment in New York or Paris or London. Her occasional affairs keep her entertained but don't disturb her lifestyle. She's no sentimental fool. After breaking off a relationship, she casually lights a cigarette and contemplates the scene outside the window of her studio.

Oh good, the color of the meat looks much better now. Only a few places are still obstinately raw. But the rest is golden brown and smells delicious. Will it be enough for the two of us? It's beginning to look pretty small.

If I were to fix myself up right now, put on one of those outfits from my trousseau and go out on the town, what would happen? Maybe an older man would approach me, with a car and everything. Mature. Retired. The only kind who can afford the luxury of being out on the prowl nowadays.

What the heck is going on here? This darn meat is starting to give off a horrible black smoke. I should have turned it over! Burned on one side. Thank goodness it has two.

Miss, if you would allow me. . . . That's Mrs.! And I warn you that my husband is a very jealous man. . . . Then he shouldn't let you go out alone. You're a temptation to any wayfaring stranger. No one in the world says "wayfaring stranger." Pedestrian, maybe? Only the newspapers when they talk about somebody who's been run over. You are a temptation for any X. Silence. Sig-ni-fi-cant. Sphinx-like stares. The older man follows me at a respectable distance. Better for him. Better for me because right around the corner, voilá! My husband, who is spying on me, who doesn't leave me alone day or night, who is suspicious of everything and everyone, Your Honor. I can't live like this; I want a divorce.

And now what? This meat's mother didn't teach it that it was meat and that it should behave properly. It rolls up just like a twist of taffy. Anyway I don't know where all that smoke keeps coming from, since I turned off the stove ages ago. Of course, of course, Dear Abby. What I must do now is open a window, turn on the air purifier, so it won't smell so bad when my husband comes home. And I'll meet him at the door all decked out, wearing my best dress, my prettiest smile, and my most cordial invitation to go out to dinner.

That's one possibility. We'll examine the menu while a miserable piece of carbonized meat lies abandoned in the depths of the garbage can. I'll be very careful not to mention the incident and will be very considerate, like a slightly irresponsible wife with an inclination toward flightiness, but not a total air-head. This is my first public appearance and I must forever live with its consequences, however imprecise.

There's another possibility. Not to open the window, not to turn on the air purifier, not to throw the meat in the garbage. And when my husband comes home, let him sniff the air, like the ogres in fairytales, and say that it smells not like human meat, but like a useless woman. I will exaggerate my repentance in order to incite him to magnanimity. After all, what happened is quite normal! What new wife doesn't experience the same thing? When we go to visit my mother-in-law, who doesn't criticize me yet because she hasn't discovered my weaknesses, she will regale me with tales of her own. Like the time her husband asked her for two eggs "over light" and she took his request literally and . . . ha, ha, ha. Did that keep her from becoming a fabulous widow—I mean, a fabulous cook? Because she became a widow later and for other reasons. From that time on, she unleashed all her maternal instincts and did nothing but spoil him. . . .

No, he is not going to be amused. He is going to say that I was not paying attention—that it is the epitome of carelessness. And, yes, I will accept his accusations with appropriate resignation.

But it's not true; it's just not true. I was paying attention to the meat the whole time, noticing all the strange things that were happening to it. No wonder Santa Teresa said that God lives among the pots and pans. Or that matter is energy or whatever it's called now.

Let us recapitulate. The piece of meat first appears with a color, a shape, and a size. Later it changes and becomes prettier and one feels very happy. Then it changes again and isn't pretty at all. And it keeps changing and changing and changing, and what one doesn't know is when to make it stop. Because if I leave the piece of meat indefinitely exposed to the fire, it will be consumed until there is nothing left of it. And the piece of meat that once gave the impression of being something so solid, so real, no longer exists.

And so? My husband also gives the impression of being solid and real when we are together, when I touch him, when I see him. Surely he changes, and I change as well, although so slowly, so gradually that neither of us realizes it. Then he leaves and abruptly becomes a memory and . . . Oh, no, I'm not going to fall into that trap: the one with the make-believe person and the make-believe narrator and the make-believe anecdote. Besides, it's not the logical conclusion that one can justly derive from the meat episode.

The meat has not ceased to exist. It has undergone a series of metamorphoses. And the fact that it is no longer perceptible to the senses does not mean that the cycle has concluded, but rather that it has simply taken the quantum leap. It will continue to function at other levels: in my consciousness, in my memory, in my will, changing me, guiding me, establishing the direction of my future.

I will be, from now on, what this moment determines I will be. Seductively confused, profoundly reserved, hypocritical. I will impose, from the beginning and with a degree of impertinence, the rules of the game. My husband will resent the thrust of my assertiveness as it gradually expands, like ripples on the water when a stone strikes its surface. He will struggle to prevail. And if he gives in, I will respond with scorn; and if he refuses, I will be unable to forgive him.

If I assume that other attitude, if I am the typical case—a woman who begs indulgence for her errors—the balance will turn in favor of my antagonist. And I will participate in the competition with a handicap that, to all appearances, predestines me to defeat and that, in the end, guarantees me triumph on the sinuous path of my humble ancestors who opened their mouths only to assent and, in doing so, won the victory for even the most irrational of their whims. The formula is old and its effectiveness is proven. If I still have doubts, I need only ask one of my neighbors. She will confirm my assertions.

It is only that I find such behavior repulsive. It is no more acceptable to me than the other option. Neither corresponds to my internal truth; neither safeguards my authenticity. Must I embrace one or the other of them, accepting their terms only because their positions are traditional and understandable to all? It's not that I am such a rare bird. One might say of me what Pfandl said of Sor Juana: that I belong to a class of brooding neurotics. The diagnosis is quite simple, but what consequences will result from assuming it?

If I insist on affirming my version of this episode, my husband will look upon me with mistrust. He is going to feel uncomfortable in my company and will live in constant fear of my being declared mentally incompetent.

Our coexistence couldn't be more problematic. And he doesn't like conflict of any sort. Much less conflicts as abstract, as absurd, as metaphysical as the ones I would pose for him. His home is a haven of peace where he takes refuge from the tempests of life. I understand that. I accepted it when I married him and was willing to sacrifice my own desires on the altar of marital bliss. But I expected my sacrifice, the complete renouncing of my personhood, to be required only on the Sublime Occasion, in the Hour of Great Resolve, in the Moment of Definitive Decision. Not in situations as insignificant and ridiculous as the one in which I find myself today. And yet . . .

Essays

To create, to speak, to think,
all in a single longed-for world
in which, one by one,
words flow along like waves in the sea.
    —Dámaso Alonso, "Voz de España"

I carry this torch from another shore
from whence I come and to which I return.
    —Gabriela Mistral, "La fervorosa"

Trills of light, strokes of words:
Abundance of anxiety. . . .
My terrestrial being . . .
Passage between two clouds,
Conscience of lightning.
    —Jorge Guillén, "Viviendo"

But all things that are reproved are made manifest by the light; for
whatever doth make manifest is light.
    —Ephesians 5:13

Like many other Spanish-American writers, Rosario Castellanos combined her task as creative artist with its complementary craft of journalism. She was a regular contributor to many journals and reviews, later collecting these essays in the volumes entitled *Juicios sumarios* (Summary Judgments; 1966) and *Mujer que sabe latín . . .* (A Woman Who Knows Latin . . . ; 1973). Two other books of her essays and articles, *El uso de la palabra* (The Use of the Word; 1974) and *El mar y sus pescaditos* (The Sea and Its Little Fishes; 1975), were compiled by friends after her death. Additional, uncollected pieces number nearly one hundred.

Throughout her life Rosario enjoyed the warm affection of a vast reading public. Already well known for her prize-winning novels, stories, and poetry, as well as her positions of responsibility at the National University, her name became a household word when she began her weekly column in Mexico City's premier newspaper, *Excélsior*.

Her studies in philosophy had developed in her a propensity for inquiry: "Concepts evoked images; splendid horizons opened before me and, without realizing it, I began to form the habit of asking questions."[1] As a result, her essays reveal a remarkable intellectual curiosity and an incisive capacity for analysis. Her insightful observations are further enhanced by the affable, conversational style that so endeared her to readers over the years.

No subject was too sensitive, too controversial, or too personal for her probing pen. Her topics range from the Mexican cultural scene to Europe, the United States, and the Middle East; from language and literature to philosophy, women's issues, art, history, politics, and the concerns of her own daily existence. She wrote with versatility and intimacy about the issues that inspired or troubled her. "Life," she wrote, "requires certain conditions to make it worthwhile. And one of these is that mankind must take an active part in community, must be a participant in its tribulations, its struggles, and its achievements."[2]

The selections that follow, all *Excélsior* articles taken from *El uso de la palabra,* provide a random sampling of her very personal perspective on reality. Sometimes nostalgic, sometimes ironic, always perceptive and thought-provoking, they reveal the heart and soul of a creative artist whose lifelong search for "el otro" had at last found an interlocutor—her reader.

In Praise of Friendship

The word "love" is used far too frequently and far too imprecisely. It moves heaven and earth, it illuminates the purest of pages, but oh, with what ease it is pressed into service to mask the most infamous of passions, the vilest selfishness, and even crime!

In order to flourish, love in any of its manifestations—even those so humble as to be found within the reach of the general populace—requires a special calling, as rare, as precise, as compelling, as that of an artist, or scholar, or saint.

Let us not speak, then, of something so complex and sublime, whose flowering is rarely favored by circumstances. Let us speak instead of another relationship to which all can aspire and all can practice: that of friendship.

According to Aristotle, friendship is one of the most rewarding necessities of life. No one could sustain life without friends, though they otherwise possess all manner of riches. In prosperity, we need friends to share the blessings we enjoy. And in suffering and sorrow, in whom can we take refuge if not in our friends?

A young man needs friends to serve as guides and counselors, confidantes and role-models. The mature man is capable of meaningful undertakings only when his actions are undergirded by the support of others. And the elderly seek strength in their time of weakness and, ultimately, in their struggle for survival, in companionship and affection.

Therefore, as we have seen, there are many and varied kinds of friendship, among which certain levels may be established.

According to this same Aristotle, types of friendship may be distinguished according to the origin of the relationship. If self-interest is the motivating force, as is frequently the case with the elderly, or pleasure, as is customarily true for youth, friendship may not be considered solid, stable, or true. Between one friend and another, the object which brings satisfaction intervenes and usurps the place of the person. And as soon as the need is satisfied or the search for pleasure is directed toward another, the union is broken. With what fear, with what repugnance, with what surprise will two beings regard one another, having been together but without truly knowing each other, without having ever achieved a true sense of intimacy!

Perfect friendship, the Greek continues, is that exhibited by men of integrity, who share a concept of virtue, and who desire only good for one another.

This shift in the center of gravity from "I" to "we" can only be realized by those who have long practiced self-discipline and the mastery of their passions—those who have directed their attention and focused it on others to the point of discovering behind appearances and actions (always enigmatic and obscure) and contradictions the ultimate authenticity that lives in the depths of every human soul. To be able to identify oneself at that level of commitment is not a feat accomplished in an instant. Even if there is love at first sight, there is no friendship that does not demand time and space to reach its perfection. The ancient proverb states, and rightly so, that two friends cannot truly know each other without having first shared a bag of salt.

Friendship is easy for two persons who are alike, but it can turn them into opposites. The superior one lowers himself in order to find a common ground with his friend, and the inferior one, spurred by the longing for companionship, is determined to ascend to the other's plane to share with him liberty and light.

Friends dislike being apart. Separation, says Emily Dickinson, is all the Hell we need. Each shared moment is precious. And the only ones who can remember the hour of loneliness are those who survive it.

The one we choose, not only with our hearts but also with our understanding, is singular and unique. And the friendship tends to endure because an entire lifetime would not be enough to assay the merits of our friend, to respond to his goodness, to bestow upon him the abundance of generous feelings he inspires in us.

But let us not deceive ourselves by thinking that this exclusive condition of friendship means isolation. On the contrary. He who has a friend lavishes benevolent actions on those around him. Those closest to us are the first to fall under the shower of gifts and liberality of our spirit, in spite of the fact that their closeness tends to make them the most irritating to us, or the most troublesome, or the most difficult to respect. Veneration of our parents is seen in this light, not as an obligation difficult to fulfill, but rather as an easy inclination of our affection. We gratefully remember what we owe them: our existence, thanks to the love they expressed to one another; the care with which they watched our growth; and the gentleness and skill with which they guided us toward independence, responsibility, and the ability to make wise choices. This entire process has as its logical consequence our zeal to know the world, to learn of it with all our senses and refined sensitivities, and to interpret it with the laws of our intelligence. And, after situating ourselves within this familiar world, to occupy our rightful place to carry out the task we have chosen for ourselves.

Brotherhood is not an instinct. Blood, contrary to popular belief, has no voice. We do not accept a brother as a given fact of nature, or as biological destiny; instead, we choose him. There are analogous points from which this relationship germinates. There are common circumstances in our development that draw us closer. But only a determination to care deeply transforms this series of coincidences into necessary reality, carried to its ultimate ends.

Children, because of their helplessness, evoke our tenderness. But we must give them more than that: a vigilant sense of responsibility, an exquisite equilibrium between the extremes of exercising our authority and respecting their freedom. There is no greater satisfaction than a child who, when grown and at the age of accountability, is able to forgive us.

Outside the family circle, friendship evolves into good will. In the workplace this allows us to manage without despotism, and to follow orders without resentment. In society we will learn to intervene without violence, but also without servility. And we will be able to look beyond the geographical borders of our own country, our customs, our race, our religious beliefs, and our political ideology to see that humanity is an attribute of all mankind.

11 January 1964

Man of Destiny

You may not be interested in hearing it, but I want to talk about it. To talk about them, rather: the forty-five years (exactly the number I have lived) as of today. I don't want to hide anything or misrepresent the date, like one covers up a gray hair or a wrinkle. No, each day has been worth what it has cost, and much more.

Because I have often resisted the frivolous temptations of false youth and because I have frequently had to force myself to go forward and fulfill the expectations of my years, I now confess my age openly and publicly. And if I were asked what has been the most important, most decisive event of my life, I could not define it as a book I read or wrote, or as a great love, or the realization of a worthy vocation, or blossoming motherhood, or the widened horizons of travel, or the acquaintance of exemplary men and women.

Yes, it is true that all this has been granted me, and I do not underestimate for a moment its importance and its impact. But I have been given more. Possibilities were available to me, doors were opened to me, all because of one government official's concept of justice and the consistency of his desire to see the law equally applied. I refer to Lázaro Cárdenas.

His was the first name I heard my elders pronounce with fear, rage, and impotence. Not only were his policies damaging to their economic interests (he ordered a redistribution of lands throughout the Republic and did not make Chiapas an exception) but those policies were also stripping them of the security they had depended on for centuries.

The world they lived in, and presumed to be both lawful and eternal, quickly crumbled. The dogmas that had long resisted the most heated debates suddenly degenerated into prejudice and sophisms that even the most inexperienced attempted to refute. The norms of conduct that had been considered more than valid, even unique, became objects of reproach and derision.

The landowners left the area, compelled not so much by poverty (since a prudent administration safeguarded them forever from the whims of fate) but by the annihilation of the symbol they had embodied. There on their land, on their property, in their dominions, they were lords of the manor; their forefathers had made history, and their descendants would come after them to protect the privilege. Their servants obeyed them, their equals respected them, the powerful sought their allegiance and their counsel.

But here in the city, they lacked relevance, got lost in the crowd, became like everyone else. And when anyone did take note of them, it was to laugh at their eccentric dress, their outdated speech, their timid and awkward demeanor.

Anonymity was both the bitterest cup and the safest refuge. Though their pride was irreparably damaged, their vanity, at least, remained intact.

Having abandoned all hope for themselves, our elders turned their thoughts to us, the younger generation. What would be our future—a future which heretofore had been a mere series of steps in a ritual and which now was exposed to attacks by the unexpected, to blows of fate, struggles against adversity?

What was to become of me? Before Cárdenas there would have been no doubt. In my childhood I would have attended sessions at our "friend's" house for her to teach me the basics of the alphabet and the four mathematical operations, and when she noticed the first signs of puberty she would have hurried me to complete the required drawing of the world map on a sheet of construction paper so she could promote me to "señorita" status.

A "señorita" was expected go on outings accompanied by her girlfriends and chaperoned by a respected person. She would receive passionate glances from timid suitors, refuse the pack of gum that the most daring would try to offer her, and she would hide in her bodice the letter (copied word for word from *The Handbook for Lovers* with a few grammatical errors here and there) given her by her favorite.

A "señorita" would go to dances after offering a novena to the miraculous Saint Caralampio so that he would assure her of not being left seated while the marimba played its languid songs, because that would have been the ultimate humiliation and an ominous sign of predisposition to spinsterhood.

A "señorita" would marry, according to her parents' wishes, a more or less close relative, owner of a ranch bordering her own, thereby providing even greater cause for rejoicing over the couple's bright prospects.

A new wife would wake up the next morning, wearing low-heeled shoes, a nondescript housedress, no makeup, and wrapped in a black shawl as befitting her new civil status. She had been transformed, actually overnight, from a desirable woman to a respectable "señora."

A respectable "señora" would have a baby every year and would entrust her offspring to Indian *nanas,* just as she entrusted the household duties to a retinue of servants who labored eagerly in the kitchen, the patios, the bedrooms, and the parlors.

The "señora," whose perpetual pregnancy limited her exercise and whose progressive obesity reduced her to complete immobility, would dictate orders, mete out punishments, enumerating her decrees from a hammock (when the weather permitted) or from her bed (when more cover was needed).

The "señora," who was not able to accompany her husband on his inspection trips to oversee his estates, would resign herself to being replaced there by a woman of a class so low as to be almost nonexistent. As a matriarch, the "señora" would take charge of the children conceived in these illicit but semipermanent unions and would find them jobs—lowly, of course, but secure situations—within the society that she governed.

The "señora" would, in time, concern herself with the boys' careers, the girls' marriages, and the equal distribution of their inheritances. Before long she would become a grandmother and, when widowhood came, it allowed her to consecrate herself fully to the church and to die with an air of sanctity.

This was the paradise that I lost "thanks to Cárdenas." These are the benefits I was never able to enjoy. Perhaps—abomination of abominations—I would have to work and, as much as we deplored the prospects, it was better to be prepared: to study for a useful career—one that would not degrade my femininity, however. A secretary? A pharmacist? In short, something that would allow me to make a living without giving me the reputation of a know-it-all, because not even my most forgiving cousins or the most snobbish social climbers—those to whom Cárdenas gave wings—would forgive me for that.

The fact is, they didn't forgive me for it. And when the time comes to evaluate the two lifestyles (the one Cárdenas made impossible and the other one Cárdenas made possible), I don't know which would have been happier, calmer, or more exempt from unexpected upheavals. But I do know that the life I have led has been the most responsible, the most meaningful, and the most humane. And I also know to whom I must extend my thanks.

30 May 1970

Women's Lib, Here

The march, organized by women in the United States to commemorate the fiftieth anniversary of their right to vote and to demand that this civic equality be extended to include equality of treatment at all levels of human interaction, occurred at the designated time and place and attracted a greater number of participants than its most optimistic promoters could have imagined.

The march, as you know, was not only to express their dissatisfaction but also to begin a strike against household chores—those jobs so *sui generis,* so unique that they are only noticed when left undone; those jobs so far removed from all laws of economics that they have either no remuneration at all or only such room, board, and clothing as their recipient deigns to provide; those jobs that, like certain very refined forms of torture administered in infamous prisons, have to be repeated soon after they are done. The march was also accompanied by a series of symbolic acts—like throwing certain pieces of women's apparel into trash cans, along with certain feminine beauty products that, if they accomplish anything, do so with scant effectiveness, in spite of their inordinate cost in both money and time—and by a number of acts of violence, such as throwing rocks at stores that sell magazines portraying women as mere sex objects or forcing their way into places reserved exclusively for men (like bars with signs on their doors like Toby's in *Little Lulu* that reads: "No women allowed").

Naturally I—since I especially enjoy this type of thing—have followed the unfolding of the whole process and have been greatly amused by the reaction of certain anti-feminists who, for lack of a more contemporary argument, have cited an event that, if it occurred at all, occurred thousands of years ago: the fact that man, according to these misled philosophers, had the generosity to relinquish one of his ribs so that we women might be created.

In the first place, no one asked his permission to carry out this operation. Secondly, when the operation took place man was in such a state of complete unconsciousness that, when he awoke, he got the surprise of the century—yea, of all time—the discovery at his side of this seductive creature who, in time, would be the cause of his leaving paradise. This creature who never ceases to beat her breast in repentance for such an error but who guards in that same breast, scarred by *mea culpa,* the inextinguishable flame of gratitude to the one who gave her life. And a life that, such as it is, many think could not be better.

But this discussion is Byzantine, as you have already realized, and so we must conclude it, since Byzantium is no longer in vogue. Let us move on to another topic, one far more significant than those we have mentioned: the repercussion that these events have caused among those who serve as spokesmen of public opinion in Mexico.

Of course, there have been commentaries. And, of course, the gamut of these commentaries has been exactly what one might expect. From foolish outbursts and impudent plays on words to the rending of garments in the face of this new apocalyptic sign that heralds the decadence and perhaps even the death of our civilization and culture.

From the "bravo" and "hooray" of some enthusiastic *congénere* to the sympathy of some member of the sex that is now more than ever the opposite one, sympathy that I applaud as heroic because I am aware of the quantity and quality of inner resistance he must overcome in order to express himself objectively. From irrational repudiation to condescending benevolence—of the sort one expresses when observing the vain efforts made by quadrupeds attempting to stand as long as possible on two feet.

The commentaries have been bitter, sweet, and buttery. But all (except for one we will mention later) have one characteristic in common: all speak of this movement for the liberation of women in the United States as if it were happening in the remotest corner of the earth or among the most exotic and incomprehensible inhabitants of the least explored planet in the universe. As if what is happening on the other side of the Río Grande had absolutely nothing to do with us.

It is understandable for us to take this position when referring to the blacks, the Chicanos, or the war in Vietnam. Our situation is totally different, and these kinds of problems don't happen here. But when it comes to women . . .

There are always those who, when looking across the river and enumerating the struggles for emancipation of many minority groups, simply add this new nucleus of combatants to the list. And if they relate it to Mexico at all, it is only to advise our politicians to take advantage of the general unrest beyond our borders and turn it to our own advantage. Since "the colossus" is revealing its feet of clay, let's see if we can't be clever enough to sell our tomatoes at a better price. Which is all well and good. But it is not enough.

Because it so happens that, as Samuel Ramos says, we are mimetic beings par excellence. And if we have imitated all the other movements, why shouldn't we imitate this one? Are there no women among us? Are they so overcome by the smoke of abnegation as to be unaware of the condition of their own lives?

Could it be that, as in the case of the appearance of the Virgin of Guadalupe, which occurred here and nowhere else, feminine nature in this country is such that it has been able to find satisfaction for all its needs and opportunities for all its potential in a society structured like today's? Could it be that their patience is guaranteed to endure forever? Could it be that they are so sensitive to ridicule that they prefer degradation?

I don't generally like to play the role of prophetess, but this is one instance that moves me to try my hand at it (apart from the fact that prophesying is one of the few jobs considered appropriate for hysterical women like yours truly). And I warn you that we Mexican women are taking due note of what is happening to our northern cousins and making ready for the day it becomes necessary for us. Perhaps not today, nor even tomorrow. Because being parasites (for that is what we are, more so than victims) has its special charm. But when the industrial development of our country obliges us to go to work in factories and offices and to care for a household and children and our appearance and our social lives, etc., etc., etc., then we, too, shall be forced into action. When the last maid—that comfortable cushion on which our conformity now rests—disappears from the scene, the first flaming rebel will make her appearance.

5 September 1970

Genesis of an Ambassador

If you, dear reader (yes, you; don't be bashful and don't try to hide because I know that you exist) were hoping that I would discuss—here in this space that *Excélsior* places at my disposal each day—the Sun and the Moon and the abstract problems of the development of syllogism or any other topic that holds little interest for me, then you are sadly mistaken. And don't blame me. Because I've been at this long enough to realize that my column is like a mirror—a little mirror to which each Saturday I pose the question of who is the most marvelous woman on the planet. And, just like in the fairy tale, it always answers "Snow White."

But that doesn't matter. I persist. And one day, out of the blue, it slips and tells me that it is I, who—as you already know, thanks to all the mass communications media—have just been reborn for the umpteenth time.

Because this matter of being born is such an important, such a transcendental act; and yet it requires such effort, such labor, and such discomfort that most people are satisfied with having done it only once in a lifetime. I, on the other hand, am one of the few who found it to be an event so marvelous as to bear repeating. Besides, repetition does bring with it the remote hope of perfection.

Because in my particular case, my first appearance in the world was rather unsettling for the spectators—a fact which, as one might expect, was also frustrating for me. As it turned out, I was not a boy (which is what brings joy to families), but instead a little girl. Red and squalling at first, toddling and smiling later, I was never able to justify my existence. Let's not even mention virtues like beauty, or grace. I didn't even resemble any ancestor—like those who, because they remember us in their wills, are always remembered with a sigh.

My own contribution? Nothing. When I started to talk, what did I say? The customary babblings and those not even poorly enough pronounced to provide laughter for those charged with caring for me and guiding my development.

Nor was I in the least cooperative. I refused food, exercise to strengthen my body, breathing fresh air, and playing the innocent games of childhood.

When I came to my senses I realized that I was on the wrong track. And that if I continued along that path I would cease to be considered merely superfluous (which I already was) and would move into the category of eliminable.

Of course I am speaking in a figurative sense. No one—in a house as large as ours and with so many people coming and going that their presence was hardly noted—was going to go to the trouble to kill me. But neither was anyone going to bother to give me any attention. The way things were going I was the perfect candidate for nothingness.

I tried what all children try in their desire to be noticed: tantrums and every sort of illness I could dream up. But since these were not successful, I found myself obliged to seek other means. And so it was that I came to write and publish my first verses. At ten years of age I was already perfectly installed as a poetess.

It was as if I had been born again—but what a spectacle! My schoolmates laughed at my rhymes as much as my rhythms. And the boys avoided my presence like they would've Medusa's, since they imagined my head to be a paralyzing mass of snakes.

I feigned conformity, anointing, but in my heart there was despair. Like the character in Garcilaso's *Ecloque,* I would not have wanted to change my condition, just my luck. To exchange with that of a vampiress, for example, like the ones who go along leaving behind them a trail of the bodies of men who have killed themselves in the wake of unrequited passion.

I suffered the metamorphosis of adolescence with the secret desire that in the end (like at the end of a tunnel) I would find myself with the seductive image of a *femme fatale.* And I even attempted to help my transformation along by shaving my head to see if something marvelous would burst forth that would not suggest macabre ideas to those who looked at me.

Well . . . I'll tell you. After many goings and comings that (like a squirrel's) were to no avail, after the aforementioned physiological, vocational, and emotional crises, I was born once more. A poetess like before, only now a little less skinny and with hair I could braid, although with a myopia worthy of a reader far more assiduous than I was then.

I can say with Amado Nervo that "I loved and was loved and the sun caressed my face." But all of that happened in the School of Philosophy and Letters, in the halls that led from one classroom to another, from a lesson poorly noted, from a tutorial en route to a professional degree.

Since all these loves fell by the wayside, I decided to make amends, that is, be born anew. This time *sub specie mysthica.* I tied up my hair, threw away all my cosmetics, and headed for Chiapas to work among the Indians.

I was happy there, as happy as a woman without children can be. But in order to have a child I had to be born once again. I unfastened my hair, put on contact lenses, and bought a new wardrobe. In fact, I did everything that animals do when they want to perpetuate the species. And need I tell you in detail all I had to go through, all the failures I had to endure? And of course you know that in giving birth to Gabriel, I gave birth to myself as a mother—a role for which I was unprepared but which I try to carry out as best I can.

Mother and poetess do not rhyme, but they go together rather well. And suddenly another incarnation: an administrative position at the National University under the presidency of Dr. Chávez. At first faltering, then slowly gaining experience, and security, at last. Exactly the moment when Dr. Chávez found it necessary to resign, leaving those of us who had been his coworkers to seek other means of support.

I was reincarnated as a professor of literature in Mexico and abroad. I was uncertain at first, but finally made a niche for myself. And now, all of a sudden, they have named me ambassador. Another task, other horizons, a new life. I accepted because—as I said before—I adore being born. And because I have confidence not so much in my own abilities as in the generosity of everyone else.

20 February 1971

A World of Change

Last Tuesday I went to the Lod airport with Gabriel, who was on his way to Mexico to spend a month of his vacation there. That's how he maintains his contacts and nurtures the substance of his own roots. This necessity (which was previously a luxury) can now be satisfied on a regular basis, thanks to new laws favoring those of us who work in the Foreign Service.

The last hours that Gabriel and I spent together were filled with tension. We are nervous and although neither of us mentions the Japanese plane that has just been hijacked, then taken on a Kafkian odyssey, and finally blown up in Libya, we both think about the risk we are taking. Is it worth it?, I ask myself. And I respond that it is not good for man to be alone, as we are assured in the first pages of Genesis. And that Gabriel, who is about to become a man, who is already beginning to be one, needs masculine role models (to imitate or reject) that I cannot provide for him. I simply give him what I have: freedom. Let him fly, let him go to be with his family and friends, let him learn from these adventures and challenges.

All very neat and very moral. But, oh, how it hurts. And since I choose not to recognize this feeling, I am irritable and become angry when the zipper on the suitcase gets stuck, when Israel Maya is sick, and the taxi that was to take us to the airport doesn't fulfill its obligation, and at six in the morning. Gabriel and I are like a couple of shipwrecked sailors hoping for some improbable ship to come and take us to our destination. We get there at last, and Gabriel boards the plane that is about to take off. He has nothing to read, but in Amsterdam, where he makes his first stop, he'll have time to look for something.

In the meantime I return to the embassy, feeling as terrible as I look: bleary-eyed, faint from hunger, and asking myself if the Bible says anything about its being good or bad for woman to be alone. Besides, my makeup has dissolved in perspiration.

I sit at my desk and with my pen I scribble shapeless forms, idle drawings. Until suddenly it all starts centering on one point, one moment, one theme: Gabriel. Not the one who has just left, but another more remote, whom—if you will indulge me—I will reflect upon a bit.

Gabriel is three years old and events pass through his consciousness without leaving an impression. That is why I am writing these lines—to give those memories the substance he cannot yet give them. That way, when he grows up and wants to count his assets, he will find a complete listing and will thus be able to review the totality of his life with one sweeping glance.

As is our custom, we have gone to Cuernavaca for the weekend. Gabriel has spent the day splashing around in the pool that is shallow enough for his size. Later he has run through the garden, playing hide-and-seek behind the trunk of each tree and flowerpot.

It is summertime, and it takes so long for night to fall that the moon dares to peep out when the sun has not completely set. Gabriel, unfamiliar with the evening sky, cries out in wonder at the sight of a star whose beauty leaves him speechless. Then I whisper in his ear the word "moon," and suddenly this far away, brilliant, heavenly creation is his.

Never has his astonishment been so enduring and so profound. And just as the moon that he beholds reflects the light of the sun, so the face of my child shines from its remote splendor. What I see before me is a light whose source is born in a space I cannot comprehend and an age I cannot fathom.

Suddenly Gabriel's eyes open wide in surprise, filled with alarm and tears of sadness: the moon has disappeared behind a dark cloud.

I realize that now, for the first time, Gabriel's consciousness has been pierced by the awareness of death. He begins to understand that the more he tries to cling to what he loves and possesses, the more things slip like sand between his fingers.

His world, which was once so solid and so true, suddenly becomes a procession of furtive images, drawn along by the endless rush of the current. All that can be rescued is what is stored in rememberings, but memory is nothing more than a brief crystallization of time that time itself dissolves and unravels. And the names with which we attempt to detain the ephemeral are but leaves that a great wind snatches from the tree and carries far, far away.

Gabriel's face, more serious now because of what he has learned, turns to me as if searching for some magic spell to recapture his primeval innocence, his paradise of certainty and immortality. But I have only words that speak of the nakedness of fire—fire that grows and diminishes before our very eyes, agonizing wildly before being extinguished and announcing its birth with joyful crackling. And words that denounce the hypocrisy of the stone that in its coldness tries to give us the illusion of immutability.

Therefore, I speak only to welcome Gabriel to our world of change, of appearances and disappearances, of shadows, of echoes, of voices, and of tangible —yet never definitive—obscurities.

Here we all go, as if on a journey, as if in a dream. From our coming to our going, and from our going to whatever lies ahead, there is no room for nostalgia.

"Look," I say to Gabriel, pointing to the moon that continues on its way, far beyond the shadow of the cloud.

And Gabriel looks. Solemnly. Because it is now another moon, and he is now another boy. And I am only a mother, who can give her son no more than she herself possesses: a bit of truth, which is like the salt that remains after the tears have gone. Salt that stings when rubbed into an open wound. Salt that seasons the food that sustains our being.

Tel Aviv, 28 August 1973

Sheer Diplomacy

One is here in her little world of "yes ma'am," sitting on her little powder keg minding her own business (except that she makes everything her business) when all of a sudden—boom!—an explosion in Cyprus. What do you think of that? To begin with, we need to alter our whole repertoire of preconceived notions and prefabricated ideas and be ready to articulate others that are a little more in keeping with reality.

Let's see: what images come to mind at the mention of the word "diplomacy"? Since you can give me only silence for an answer—which I can understand—I will go on to tell you the images that come to my mind: Lawrence Durrell's "Mountolive," uniformed and decorated, descending the main staircase of his palace in Cairo on his way to search for adventure. He assumed various roles: that of "Justine," whose frivolity hid a complex intrigue of espionage; that of "Baltasar," who founded a circle of scholars from the cabbala so as not to arouse suspicions about other more offensive activities; that of the English official, who, finding himself in the position of denouncing his friends in order to be faithful to his country, chose an unexpected solution: suicide. An air of mystery, a masked ball, an attempt at literature that is disdainfully left aside in a notebook because there are much more important issues to resolve.

Is that what they call "the golden exile"? Of course not, Peyrefitte wrathfully responds. Embassies are nothing but whitewashed sepulchres. Behind the elegant facade lies decadence, and behind the impeccable structure, vulgarity. "The situation is so grave," he announces with a great apocalyptic shout, "that we find ourselves nearing 'The End of the Embassy Age.'"

Now let me add my little grain of sand. Even with all their boldness and accomplishment, neither Lawrence Durrell nor Peyrefitte commanded the kitchen, which is where—I speak as a woman—the crux of the matter is found.

Frequently it is necessary to give a dinner party. Seated? Naturally. It was with that objective that this house was rented. Because the others, although they were better located and prettier and more comfortable and much, much cheaper, didn't have that archaeological piece of furniture known in these parts as the dining table. It seats twelve. One more would be bad luck. Two more would be financial disaster.

What's the first step? A tentative guest list, because someone will already have a previous engagement, and another will have a toothache, and yet another will have a problem finding a date, and that upsets the balance of things—which is not allowed. And that is where yours truly comes in. When I first arrived here I was surprised by my colleagues' frequent insistence that I dine in their company—until I began to put two and two together. Once it fell my lot to be seated next to the ambassador of Costa Rica who, being a priest, was celibate. Since then the list has been more varied. I provide companionship not only for bachelors, but for full-time or part-time widowers as well. But do not be misled, as I once was. They always place us at an appropriate distance, which will allow the table to have a geometric design of the utmost intricacy and precision.

After the most experienced strategists have racked their brains to devise all the combinations possible to satisfy the exigencies of protocol, of rank, and of priority so that no two men who might initiate a conspiracy will be seated next to each other, and, even worse, that any two women who might begin a gossip session will be kept apart—we proceed to the next step, which is the elaboration of the menu.

Into the chancery comes Mrs. Weichert. She is in charge of providing services, and those who want visas fall on their knees before her, explaining their problems and begging her to solve them. Others ask for her autograph, and some are content with a snapshot. Accustomed to such tribute, which she owes to her distinguished bearing, her impeccable coiffure, and that air—both majestic and benevolent—which is the privilege of aristocracy, she smiles.

I don't go out to greet Mrs. Weichert, since comparison is so distasteful. I wait for her in my office, where I am subjected to her interrogation.

"May I know who the guests will be?"

At first I stated the facts, *ipso facto*. But now, after sending many telegrams in code, I have learned to be more cautious.

"Does it really matter?"

"It is essential. If we invite businessmen, they have ulcers, and we must choose certain dishes to the exclusion of others. If it is a group of intellectuals, they're always hungry, so we must concentrate more on quantity than quality."

"This time the dinner is going to be in honor of Minister X," I revealed.

"Oh, then a bland diet is in order, since the Minister has just gotten false teeth."

With my fate in such capable hands, what could go wrong? The usual. At a quarter till twelve, one of the guests has a mishap, making it impossible for him to come, and the whole house of cards, so carefully stacked, comes tumbling down. It is then that I resort to my pinch-hitter. The man of the house: Gabriel.

But he is well aware that his dignity is on the line, and he does not readily agree. I must rely on emotional blackmail, like any typical, self-sacrificing Mexican mother, and I must appeal to his patriotic duty. But he wants specific details. Who will sit next to him at the table? Trembling, since I realize the predicament we are in, and playing my last card, I tell him:

"One of the ladies is from Chile and went into exile during Allende's presidency. The other one was born in South Africa. But (I am quick to add) you needn't discuss apartheid or mention the military junta."

"I won't bring it up . . . but I'm not going to keep quiet if they provoke me."

"You don't have to keep quiet. Just change the subject."

"How do you do that?"

"Easy. If they tell you, for example, that apartheid is justified by the blacks' natural inferiority, as evidenced by the inferior quality of their work, which is fundamentally agricultural, you say, matter-of-factly, that crops depend mainly on the rains, and that this year there's been a drought, or some floods—it doesn't matter what, there's always something. And you go from there."

"And what about Allende?"

"They will complain about how agrarian reform was a disaster, about the scanty harvests . . . and then you bring up the drought and the floods again. You know what I think? English culture's greatest contribution to human coexistence is the discovery of the weather as a topic of conversation."

Tel Aviv, 6 August 1974

Because I could not stop for death—
He kindly stopped for me—
The carriage held but just Ourselves—
And Immortality.
        —Emily Dickinson, "712"

And those who transcend do not die,
    they illuminate.
And their work remains,
    burning like a lamp.
        —Oscar Bonifaz, Rosario

Notes

INTRODUCTION

1. Carlos Pellicer, in *A Rosario Castellanos: sus amigos* (México: Año Internacional de la Mujer/Programa de México, 1975), 40. This and subsequent quoted passages from the Spanish are my translation.

2. Carlos Monsiváis, "Apuntes para una declaración de fe (sobre la poesía de Rosario Castellanos)," *Siempre!* 28 August 1974, 2.

3. Rosario Castellanos, *Juicios sumarios* (Xalapa, México: Universidad Veracruzana, 1966), 135. Hereafter cited in the text as *Juicios*.

4. Günter W. Lorenz, "Rosario Castellanos," in his *Diálogo con Latinoamérica* (Santiago de Chile: Editorial Pomaire, 1972), 208.

5. María Rosa Fiscal, *La imagen de la mujer en la narrativa de Rosario Castellanos* (México: Universidad Nacional Autónoma de México), 1980, 104.

6. Rosario Castellanos, *El uso de la palabra* (1974; reprint, México: Editores Mexicanos Unidos, 1982), 211. Hereafter cited in the text as *El uso*.

7. Walter Langford, *The Mexican Novel Comes of Age* (Notre Dame, Ind.: University of Notre Dame Press, 1971), 83.

8. Lorenz, "Rosario Castellanos," 194.

9. María Luisa Cresta de Leguizamón, "En recuerdo de Rosario Castellanos," *La Palabra y el Hombre*, no. 19 (July-September 1976): 4.

10. Castellanos, in an interview with Emmanuel Carballo in his *Diecinueve protagonistas de la literatura mexicana del siglo XX* (México: Empresas Editorial, 1963), 422.

11. Margarita García Flores, "El libro y la vida: *Los convidados de agosto*," *El Día*, 29 August 1964, 9.

12. Carballo, *Diecinueve protagonistas*, 422.

13. Beth Miller and Alfonso González, *Veinte y seis autoras del México actual* (México: B. Costa-Amic, 1978), 135.

14. Rosario Castellanos, "Prólogo," in Susan Francis, *Habla y literatura popular en la antigua capital chiapaneca* (México: Instituto Nacional Indigenista, 1960), 5.

15. *Caxlán* is apparently an Indian version of *castellano*, or Castilian (Spanish), used exclusively by Indians to refer to non-Indians; roughly the equivalent of Ladino or white.

16. Lorenz, "Rosario Castellanos," 210.

17. Rosario Castellanos, *Poesía no eres tú: obra poética 1948–1971*, 2d ed. (México: Fondo de Cultura Económica, 1975), 293. Hereafter cited in the text as *Poesía*.

18. Elena Poniatowska, "¡Te hicieron parque, Rosario!" *Revista de Bellas Artes*, no. 18 (November–December 1971): 2.

19. Carballo, *Diecinueve protagonistas,* 412.

20. Elena Poniatowska, "Rosario Castellanos, las letras que quedan de tu nombre," *La Cultura en México,* supl. de *Siempre!* 4 September 1974, 6.

21. Nahum Megged, "Entre soledad y búsqueda de diálogo" in "Homenaje a Rosario Castellanos 1925–1974," *Los Universitarios* 15–31 (August 1974): 4.

22. Beatriz Reyes Nevares, *Rosario Castellanos* (México: Departamento Editorial Secretaría de la Presidencia, 1976), 20.

23. María Luisa Mendoza, "Taladrada en el hilo de Rosario," *Excélsior,* 6 April 1958, 3.

24. Beatriz Espejo, "Entrevista con Rosario Castellanos," in *A Rosario Castellanos: sus amigos,* 22.

25. Mendoza, "Taladrada," 3.

26. It was a custom in Chiapas for the children of wealthy Ladinos to have live-in Indian playmates their own age. These Indian children served as living playthings and often had to bear the brunt of their master's or mistress's ill humor or cruel whims.

27. After the death of her younger brother, Mario Benjamín, for whom her parents showed a decided preference, Rosario's feelings of rejection were intensified. When the government closed the private schools and took over the educational system, her parents removed her from school and provided her education at home. She was shut in a room filled with books. Now an only child, she was overprotected and carefully guarded. Her parents preferred to see her reading for hours on end than to allow her out of the house.

28. Elena Poniatowska in her Prologue to Rosario Castellanos, *Meditación en el umbral: antología poética* (México: Fondo de Cultura Económica, 1985), 26–27.

29. Sor Juana Inés de la Cruz, *Poesía, teatro y prosa,* ed. Antonio Castro Leal, 7th ed. (México: Editorial Porrúa, 1976), 34.

30. *Los narradores ante el público,* vol. 1 (México: Joaquín Mortiz, 1966), 93.

31. Rosario Castellanos, *Mujer que sabe latín . . .* (1973; reprint, México: Fondo de Cultura Económica, 1984), 206. The title of this book is taken from a Spanish proverb and concludes with the words "ni halla marido, ni halla buen fin" (A woman who knows Latin neither finds a husband nor comes to a good end). Hereafter cited in the text as *Mujer.*

32. Victor Baptiste, *La obra poética de Rosario Castellanos* (Ph.D. diss., University of Illinois, 1967; Santiago de Chile: Exégesis, 1972), 6.

33. Carballo, *Diecinueve protagonistas,* 420.

34. Many of these essays and articles were collected and published posthumously in the collections *El uso de la palabra* (The Use of the Word; 1974) and *El mar y sus pescaditos* (The Sea and Its Little Fishes; 1975).

35. Cresta de Leguizamón, "En recuerdo," 8.

36. Elena Poniatowska, cited by Beth Miller in *Mujeres en la literatura* (México: Fleisher Editora, 1978), 18.

37. Miller and González, *Veinte y seis autoras,* 118.

38. Cresta de Leguizamón, "En recuerdo," 8.

39. Reyes Nevares, *Rosario Castellanos,* 54.

40. Victoria E. Urbano, "La justicia femenina de Rosario Castellanos," *Letras femeninas* 1, no. 2 (1975): 13.

41. Lorenz, "Rosario Castellanos," 190.

42. Poniatowska, "Rosario Castellanos, las letras que quedan de tu nombre," 6–7.

43. Monsiváis, "Apuntes para una declaración de fe," 3.

44. Margarita García Flores, "Rosario Castellanos: la lucidez como forma de vida," *La Onda,* 6.

45. Megged, "Entre soledad," 4.

46. Carballo, *Diecinueve protagonistas,* 416.

47. Miller and González, *Veinte y seis autoras,* 135.

48. Castellanos explained:

> I married at 32, an age when I was already too accustomed to living alone, and with a demanding career. . . . Although my husband has often assisted me in carrying on my work, I fell behind in several projects in the early years of our marriage, due to two miscarriages. Besides the emotional upheavals inherent in these events, they had a serious psychological effect on me, because they brought to mind the tragic loss of my brother in my childhood. Finally, in 1961, I was successful in giving birth to a third child, who lived. (Rhoda Dybvig, *Rosario Castellanos, biografía y novelística* [México: Ediciones de Andrea, 1965. Master's thesis U.N.A.M., Dirección de Cursos Temporales, 1965], 24.)

Difficult from the beginning, Castellanos's marriage in 1958 to philosophy professor Ricardo Guerra ended in divorce. Their only son, Gabriel Guerra Castellanos, who accompanied his mother during her ambassadorial appointment in Israel, now resides in the Soviet Union, where he is Mexico's cultural attaché.

49. Dolores Cordero, "Rosario Castellanos: 'La mujer mexicana, cómplice de su verdugo,'" *Revista de Revistas,* weekly publication of *Excélsior,* 10 November 1971, 27.

50. Rosario Castellanos, *El eterno femenino* (México: Fondo de Cultura Económica, 1975), 22.

51. She stepped out of the shower in her Tel Aviv home, with feet still damp, and reaching to turn on a lamp was electrocuted by a powerful surge of current.

52. Cordero, "Rosario Castellanos," 27.

POETRY

1. Rosario Castellanos, in an interview with Emmanuel Carballo in his *Diecinueve protagonistas de la literatura mexicana del siglo XX* (México: Empresas Editorial, 1963), 412.

2. Mary Seale Vásquez, "Rosario Castellanos, Image and Idea," *Homenaje a Rosario Castellanos* (Valencia: Ediciones Álbatros Hispanófila, 1980), 20.

3. Carballo, *Diecinueve protagonistas,* 412.

4. Rosario Castellanos, *Poesía no eres tú: obra poética 1948–1971,* 2d. ed. (México: Fondo de Cultura Económica, 1975), 7. (Hereafter cited in the text as *Poesía.*)

5. Rosario Castellanos, *Juicios sumarios* (Xalapa: Universidad Veracruzana, 1966), 430. (Hereafter cited in the text as *Juicios*.)

6. Carballo, *Diecinueve protagonistas*, 413.

7. Rhoda Dybvig, *Rosario Castellanos, biografía y novelística* (México: Ediciones de Andrea, 1965), 20.

8. Carballo, *Diecinueve protagonistas*, 414.

9. Ibid., 414.

10. Rosario Castellanos, *Mujer que sabe latín . . .* (1973; reprint, México: Fondo de Cultura Económica, 1984), 207.

PROSE FICTION

1. Rosario Castellanos, in an interview with Emmanuel Carballo in his *Diecinueve protagonistas de la literatura mexicana del siglo XX* (México: Empresas Editorial, 1963), 418–19.

2. Ibid., 419.

From Balún-Canán (*The Nine Guardians*)

The title is taken from the Mayan name for the region around the town of Comitán, a region of nine (*balún*) guardian-mountains (*canán*).

1. A *tzec* is a skirt of coarse blue cloth used in Chiapas. It is very ample and is worn wrapped around the waist with heavy pleating in the front.

2. *Posol,* or *pozol,* is a lump of corn meal kneaded into a ball. The Indians wrap it in banana leaves and carry it as food on journeys. It is soaked in water to make a thick broth for drinking.

3. *Atole* is a thick drink made with corn meal and chocolate.

From Oficio de tinieblas (*Tenebrae Service*)

The title is taken from the Tenebrae Service that is part of the celebration of Good Friday. It consists of gradually extinguishing the altar candles to signify the darkness that fell over the world after the crucifixion of Jesus Christ. In Castellanos's novel, the darkness (tenebrae/tinieblas) in which the characters live and move extends its symbolism beyond the tragedy of the final chapters to include the greater one that results when individuals and racial groups are unable to live together in harmony.

ESSAYS

1. *Los narradores ante el público,* vol. 1 (México: Joaquín Mortiz, 1966), 93.

2. Rosario Castellanos, *El mar y sus pescaditos* (1975; reprint, México: Editores Mexicanos Unidos, 1982), 11.

Selected Bibliography

WORKS BY ROSARIO CASTELLANOS

Álbum de familia. 4th ed. México: Editorial Joaquín Mortiz, 1979.

Balún-Canán. 3d ed. México: Fondo de Cultura Económica, 1961.

"Baño ritual en el Grijalva." Unpublished poem given to Oscar Bonifaz, 5 November 1948.

Ciudad Real. 2d ed. Xalapa, México: Universidad Veracruzana, 1982.

El eterno femenino. México: Fondo de Cultura Económica, 1975.

El mar y sus pescaditos. 1975. Reprint. México: Editores Mexicanos Unidos, 1982.

El uso de la palabra. 1974. Reprint. México: Editores Mexicanos Unidos, 1982.

Juicios sumarios. Xalapa, México: Universidad Veracruzana, 1966.

Los convidados de agosto. 7th ed. México: Ediciones Era, 1982.

"Madre india." *El Sol de Chiapas* (Tuxtla Gutiérrez, Chiapas) 108 (28 August 1975): 3.

Meditación en el umbral: antología poética. Compiled by Julian Palley; prologue by Elena Poniatowska. México: Fondo de Cultura Económica, 1985.

Mujer que sabe latín. . . . 1973. Reprint. México: Fondo de Cultura Económica, 1984.

Oficio de tinieblas. 5th ed. México: Editorial Joaquín Mortiz, 1982.

Poesía no eres tú: obra poética 1948–1971. 2d ed. México: Fondo de Cultura Económica, 1975.

"Rosario Castellanos." *Artes Hispánicas* (New York) 1 (1967–68): 66–70.

"Tablero de damas: pieza en un acto." *América: Revista Antológica,* no. 68 (June 1972): 185–224.

"Tres nudos en la red." *Revista de la Universidad de México,* no. 8 (April 1971): 6–11. Reprint. *Antología de cuentos chiapanecos,* 7–30. Tuxtla Gutiérrez (México): Secretaría de Educación y Cultura del Gobierno del Estado de Chiapas y Programa Cultural de las Fronteras S.E.P., 1985.

WORKS ABOUT ROSARIO CASTELLANOS

A Rosario Castellanos: sus amigos. Recopilación de textos y selección poética de Ma. del Refugio Llamas. México: Año Internacional de la Mujer/Programa de México, 1975.

Baptiste, Victor. *La obra poética de Rosario Castellanos.* Ph.D. diss., University of Illinois, 1967; Santiago de Chile: Exégesis, 1972.

Bonifaz, Oscar. *Rosario.* México: Presencia Latinoamericana, 1984.

Carballo, Emmanuel. "Rosario Castellanos." In his *Diecinueve protagonistas de la literatura mexicana del siglo XX*, 411–24. México: Empresas Editorial, 1963.

Cordero, Dolores. "Rosario Castellanos: 'La mujer mexicana, cómplice de su verdugo.'" *Revista de Revistas*, weekly publication of *Excélsior*, 10 November 1971, 24–27.

Cresta de Leguizamón, María Luisa. "En recuerdo de Rosario Castellanos." *La Palabra y el Hombre*, no. 19 (July-September 1976): 3–18.

Dybvig, Rhoda. *Rosario Castellanos, biografía y novelística*. México: Ediciones de Andrea, 1965. (Master's thesis. U.N.A.M., Dirección de Cursos Temporales, 1965.)

Fiscal, María Rosa. *La imagen de la mujer en la narrativa de Rosario Castellanos*. México: Universidad Nacional Autónoma de México, 1980.

Fiscal, María Rosa, Estela Franco, Elena Poniatowska, and Eraclio Zepeda. "Homenaje a Rosario Castellanos." Panel Discussion, México, D.F., 14 August 1984.

Francis, Susan. *Habla y literatura popular en la antigua capital chiapaneca*. Introduction by Rosario Castellanos. México: Instituto Nacional Indigenista, 1960.

García Flores, Margarita. "El libro y la vida: *Los convidados de agosto*." *El Día*, 29 August 1964, 9.

———. "Rosario Castellanos: la lucidez como forma de vida." *La Onda*, supplement of *Novedades*, 18 August 1974, 6–7.

"Homenaje a Rosario Castellanos 1925–1974." *Los Universitarios*, no. 31 (15–31 August 1974): 1–8.

Langford, Walter M. "Rosario Castellanos." In his *The Mexican Novel Comes of Age*, 182–85. Notre Dame, Ind.: University of Notre Dame Press, 1971.

Leiva, Raúl. "Escaparate." *México en la Cultura*, supplement of *Novedades*, 4 December 1966, 6.

Lorenz, Günter. "Rosario Castellanos." In his *Diálogo con Latinoamérica*, 185–211. Santiago de Chile: Editorial Pomaire, 1972.

Los narradores ante el público, vol. 1. México: Joaquín Mortiz, 1966.

Mendoza, María Luisa. "Taladrada en el hilo de Rosario." *Excélsior*, 6 April 1958, 3.

Miller, Beth. *Mujeres en la literatura*. México: Fleisher Editora, 1978.

Miller, Beth, and Alfonso González. "Rosario Castellanos." In their *Veinte y seis autoras del México actual*, 115–38. México: B. Costa-Amic, 1978.

Monsiváis, Carlos. "Apuntes para una declaración de fe (sobre la poesía de Rosario Castellanos)." *Siempre!* 28 August 1974, 2–3.

Poniatowska, Elena. "Rosario Castellanos." *México en la Cultura*, supplement of *Novedades*, 26 January 1958, 7, 10.

———. "Rosario Castellanos, las letras que quedan de tu nombre." *La Cultura en México*, supplement of *Siempre!* 4 September 1974, 6–8.

———. "¡Te hicieron parque, Rosario!" *Revista de Bellas Artes*, no. 18 (November-December 1971): 2.

Reyes Nevares, Beatriz. *Rosario Castellanos*. México: Departamento Editorial Secretaría de la Presidencia, 1976.

"Rosario Castellanos. La Mujer del Año 1967." *Siempre!* 13 March 1968, 55.

Sommers, Joseph. "The Present Moment in the Mexican Novel." *Books Abroad* 40 (Summer 1966): 261–66.

Sor Juana Inés de la Cruz. *Poesía, teatro y prosa.* Edited by Antonio Castro Leal. 7th ed. México: Editorial Porrúa, 1976.

Urbano, Victoria E. "La justicia femenina de Rosario Castellanos." *Letras Femeninas* 1, no. 2 (1975): 9–20.

WORKS BY ROSARIO CASTELLANOS
IN ENGLISH TRANSLATION

Poems

"Ajedrez" (Chess). *Translation,* no. 6 (Spring 1978): 128. Translated by Maureen Ahern. Also in *Open to the Sun: A Bilingual Anthology of Latin American Women Poets,* translated by Maureen Ahern and edited by Nora Jacquez Wieser, 136–37. Van Nuys, Calif.: Perivale Press, 1979.

"Amanecer" (Dawn). In *Open to the Sun: A Bilingual Anthology of Latin American Women Poets,* translated by Maureen Ahern and edited by Nora Jacquez Wieser, 134–35. Van Nuys, Calif.: Perivale Press, 1979.

"Amor" (Love). *El corno emplumado* (The Plumed Horn), no. 18 (April 1966): 74–75. Translated by Elinor Randall.

"Autorretrato" (Self-Portrait). *Feminist Studies* 3, nos. 3–4 (Spring-Summer 1976): 63–65. Translated by Beth Miller.

"La casa vacía" (The Empty House). In *New Voices of Hispanic America: An Anthology,* translated and edited by Darwin J. Flakoll and Claribel Alegría, 119–20. Boston: Beacon Press, 1962.

"De mutilaciones" (Re: Mutilations). *Latin American Literary Review* 8, no. 15 (Fall-Winter 1979): 102–4. Translated by Maureen Ahern.

"Día inútil" (Useless Day). *Colorado State Review* 7, no. 1 (Spring 1979): 13. Translated by Maureen Ahern. Also in *Anthology of Women Poets,* edited by J. Bankier, D. Earnshaw, and D. Lashgari. New York: Macmillan Publishing Co., 1983.

"Dos meditaciones" (Two Mediatations [sic]). *Recent Books in Mexico* 6, no. 4 (May 1959): 4. Translator not given.

"Economía doméstica" (Home Economics). *Feminist Studies* 3, nos. 3–4 (Spring-Summer 1976): 62. Translated by Beth Miller. Also in *13th Moon* 4, no. 2 (1979): 12–14. Translated by Maureen Ahern.

"Elegía" (Elegy). *Caliban* 2, no. 2 (Fall-Winter 1978): 33. Translated by Maureen Ahern. Also in *Open to the Sun: A Bilingual Anthology of Latin American Women Poets,* translated by Maureen Ahern and edited by Nora Jacquez Wieser, 130–31. Van Nuys, Calif.: Perivale Press, 1979.

"Elegía del amado fantasma. Primera elegía" (First Elegy). In *The Muse in Mexico: A*

Mid-Century Miscellany, 92. Translated by Olive Senior-Ellis and edited by Thomas Mabry Cranfill. Austin: University of Texas Press, 1959.

"Se habla de Gabriel" (Speaking of Gabriel). In *Open to the Sun: A Bilingual Anthology of Latin American Women Poets*, translated by Maureen Ahern and edited by Nora Jacquez Wieser, 138–39. Van Nuys, Calif.: Perivale Press, 1979.

"Lamentación de Dido" (Dido's Lament). *Translation*, no. 5 (Spring 1978): 66–70. Translated by Julian Palley.

"Lecciones de cosas" (Learning about Things). *Latin American Literary Review* 8, no. 15 (Fall-Winter 1979): 93–99. Translated by Maureen Ahern.

"Malinche" (Malinche). *Colorado State Review* 7, no. 1 (Spring 1979): 11–12. Translated by Maureen Ahern.

"Meditación en el umbral" (Meditation on the Brink). *Caliban* 2, no. 2 (Fall–Winter 1978): 35. Translated by Maureen Ahern.

"Memorial de Tlatelolco" (Memorandum on Tlatelolco). *Caliban* 2, no. 2 (Fall–Winter 1978): 37. Translated by Maureen Ahern.

"Mirando a la Gioconda" (Looking at the Mona Lisa). *Latin American Literary Review* 8, no. 15 (Fall–Winter 1979): 104–5. Translated by Maureen Ahern.

"Monólogo de la extranjera" (Foreign Woman). In *Latin American Writing Today*, translated and edited by John Michael Cohen, 103. Harmondsworth, Middlesex: Penguin Books, 1967. Also as "Monologue of a Foreign Woman." In *Latin American Literary Review* 8, no. 15 (Fall–Winter 1979): 88–93. Translated by Maureen Ahern.

"Nazareth" (Nazareth). *Caliban* 2, no. 2 (Fall–Winter 1978), 33. Translated by Maureen Ahern. Also in *Translation*, no. 6 (Spring 1978): 127.

"El otro" (The Other). *Paintbrush*, no. 4 (Autumn 1975): 15. Translated by Mark Cramer. Also as "Someone Else" in *Open to the Sun: A Bilingual Anthology of Latin American Women Poets*, translated by Maureen Ahern and edited by Nora Jacquez Wieser, 132–33. Van Nuys, Calif.: Perivale Press, 1979.

"Una palmera" (A Palm Tree). In *The Muse in Mexico: A Mid-Century Miscellany*, translated by Olive Senior-Ellis and edited by Thomas Mabry Cranfill, 93. Austin: University of Texas Press, 1959.

"Poesía no eres tú" (Poetry Isn't You). *Latin American Literary Review* 8, no. 15 (Fall-Winter 1979): 101–2. Translated by Maureen Ahern.

"Post-Scriptum" (Post Script). *Latin American Literary Review* 8, no. 15 (Fall–Winter 1979): 99–101. Translated by Maureen Ahern.

"Privilegio del suicida" (The Suicide's Privilege). *El Corno Emplumado* (The Plumed Horn), no. 18 (April 1966): 77. Translated by Elinor Randall.

"Rutina" (Routine). *New Letters* 46, no. 1 (Fall 1979): 79. Translated by Maureen Ahern.

"Silencio cerca de una piedra antigua" (Silence Concerning an Ancient Stone). In *The Muse in Mexico: A Mid-Century Miscellany*, translated by Olive Senior-Ellis and edited by Thomas Mabry Cranfill, 94. Austin: University of Texas Press, 1959. Also as "Silence Around an Ancient Stone." In *Paintbrush*, no. 4 (Autumn 1975):

15. Translated by Mark Cramer. Also as "Silence Near an Ancient Stone." *13th Moon* 4, no. 2 (1979): 10–11. Translated by Maureen Ahern.

"Testamento de Hecuba" (Hecuba's Testament). *Atlantic Monthly,* no. 213 (March 1964): 120. Translated by John Fredrick Nims.

"Toma de conciencia" (Consciousness). *13th Moon* 4, no. 2 (1979): 15–18. Translated by Maureen Ahern.

"Tránsito" (Passage). *Translation,* no. 6 (Spring 1978): 126–27. Translated by Maureen Ahern.

"Válium 10" (Valium 10). In *Spinoza's Stone and Other Poems,* translated by Julian Palley, 77–79. New York: JNP Publishers, 1976.

Prose

Balún-Canán (The Nine Guardians). Translated by Irene Nicholson. London: Faber and Faber, 1958. Reprint. New York: Vanguard Press, 1959.

Oficio de tinieblas (Office of Tenebrae). [Fragment.] In *Latin American Literature Today,* translated by Anne Fremantle and Christopher Fremantle and edited by Anne Fremantle, 72–79. New York: Mentor, 1977.

La participación de la mujer en la educación formal (Women's Participation in Formal Education). Translators not given. México: Centro Nacional de Productividad, 1970.

"El viudo Román" (The Widower Román). *The Texas Quarterly* 16, no. 2 (June 1973): 118–66. Translated by Ruth Peacock and others.

Collections

Ahern, Maureen, ed. and trans. *Looking at the Mona Lisa.* Bradford, England: Rivelin Press and London: Ecuatorial, 1981.

———. *A Rosario Castellanos Reader.* Translated by Maureen Ahern and others. Austin: University of Texas Press, 1988.

Palley, Julian, ed. *Meditation on the Threshold.* Tempe, Ariz.: Bilingual Press (Editorial Bilingüe), 1988.

Vicuña, Cecilia, and Magda Bogin, eds. *The Selected Poems of Rosario Castellanos.* Translated by Magda Bogin. St. Paul, Minn.: Graywolf Press, 1988.

SELECTED CASTELLANOS CRITICISM IN ENGLISH

Ahern, Maureen, and Mary S. Vásquez, eds. *Homenaje a Rosario Castellanos.* Valencia: Ediciones Albatros Hispanófila, 1980.

Alarcón, Norma. "Rosario Castellanos' Feminist Poetics: Against the Sacrificial Contract." Ph.D. diss., Indiana University, 1983.

Allgood, Myralyn F. "Conflict and Counterpoint: A Study of Characters and Characterization in Rosario Castellanos' Indigenist Fiction." Ph.D. diss., University of Alabama, 1985.

———, ed. and trans. *Remembering Rosario: A Personal Glimpse into the Life and Works of Rosario Castellanos.* Potomac, Md.: Scripta Humanistica, 1990.

Anderson, Helene. "Rosario Castellanos and the Structures of Power." In *Contemporary Women Authors of Latin America,* edited by Doris Meyer and Margarite Fernández Olmos, 22–32. Brooklyn, N.Y.: Brooklyn College Press, 1983.

Benton, Gabriel von Munk. "Women Writers of Contemporary Mexico." *Books Abroad* 33 (1959): 15–19.

Brodman, Barbara Lynn C. "Historical and Literary Bases of the Mexican Cult of Death and its Manifestations in Selected Contemporary Mexican Short Stories." Ph.D. diss., University of Florida, 1974.

Brushwood, John S. *Mexico in its Novel.* Austin: University of Texas Press, 1966.

———. *The Spanish-American Novel: A Twentieth Century Survey.* Austin: University of Texas Press, 1975.

Cypress, Sandra Messenger. "Onomastics and Thematics in *Balún-Canán.*" *Literary Onomastics Studies* 13 (1986): 83–96.

Davis, Leslie. "Myth in *Oficio de tinieblas.*" Master's thesis, University of Texas, Austin, 1967.

Dorward, Frances R. "The Function of Interiorization in *Oficio de tinieblas.*" *Neophil* 69, no. 3 (July 1985): 374–85.

Dunstan, Florene. "A Comparison of Two Contemporary Novels *Balún-Canán* and *To Kill a Mockingbird.*" *Agnes Scott Alumnae Quarterly* 45, no. 2 (Winter 1967): 2–7.

———. "The Nine Guardians (*Balún-Canán*)." *The Arch* 13, no. 3 (Spring 1966): [n. pag.].

Fox-Lockert, Lucía. "Rosario Castellanos." In *Women Novelists in Spain and Spanish America,* 202–15. Metuchen, N.J., and London: Scarecrow Press, 1979.

Franco, Jean. *The Modern Culture of Latin America.* Oxford: Alden Press, 1967.

———. *Spanish American Literature since Independence.* New York: Barnes and Nobel, 1973.

Gómez Parham, Mary. "Intellectual Influences on the Works of Rosario Castellanos." *Foro Literario: Revista de Literatura y Lenguaje* 7, no. 12 (1984): 34–40.

González Peña, Carlos. *History of Mexican Literature.* Dallas: Southern Methodist University Press, 1968.

Holm, Susan Fleming. "'But Then Face to Face': Approaches to the Poetry of Rosario Castellanos." Ph.D. diss., University of Kansas, 1985.

———. "Defamiliarization in the Poetry of Rosario Castellanos." *Third Woman,* 1986, 87–97.

Jolles, A. M. "Some Dominant Themes in the Contemporary Mexican Novel: Religion, North America, and the Individual, with particular reference to novels by Rosario Castellanos, Carlos Fuentes, Juan Rulfo, Luis Spota and Agustín Yáñez." Ph.D. diss., Westfield College, University of London, 1974.

Lindstrom, Naomi. "Women's Expression and Narrative Technique in Rosario Castellanos' *In Darkness*." *Modern Language Studies* 13, no. 3 (Summer 1983): 71–80.

Loustaunau, Martha Oehmke. "Rosario Castellanos: The Humanization of the Female Character." In her "Mexico's Contemporary Women Novelists," 48–74. Ph.D. diss., University of New Mexico, 1973.

McMurray, George R. "Current Trends in the Mexican Novel." *Hispania* 51, no. 3 (1968): 532–37.

———. "The Present Moment in the Mexican Novel." *Books Abroad* 40 (Summer 1966): 261–66.

Miller, Beth. "Women and Feminism in the Works of Rosario Castellanos." In *Feminist Criticism: Essays on Theory, Poetry and Prose,* edited by Cheryl L. Brown and Karen Olson, 198–210. Metuchen and London: Scarecrow Press, 1978.

———. *Women in Hispanic Literature, Icons and Fallen Idols.* Berkeley and Los Angeles: University of California Press, 1983.

Miller, Martha LaFollette. "A Semiotic Analysis of Three Poems by Rosario Castellanos." *Revista/Review Interamericana* 12, no. 1 (Spring 1982): 77–86.

Nelson, Esther W. "Point of View in Selected Poems by Rosario Castellanos." *Revista/Review Interamericana* 12, no. 1 (Spring 1982): 56–64.

Parham, Mary Helene. "Alienation in the Fiction of Rosario Castellanos." Ph.D. diss., University of California, Los Angeles, 1979.

Robinson, George Alexander. "Indigenism and Feminism in the Prose Fiction of Rosario Castellanos." Ph.D. diss., Louisiana State University and Agricultural and Mechanical College, 1981.

Rodríguez-Peralta, Phyllis. "Images of Women in Rosario Castellanos' Prose." *Latin American Literary Review* 6, no. 11 (Fall–Winter 1977): 68–80.

"Rosario Castellanos dies: Mexican envoy to Israel." *New York Times,* 9 August 1974, 36.

Ruta, Suzanne. "Adiós, Machismo: Rosario Castellanos Goes Her Own Way." *Voice Literary Supplement,* June 1989, 33–34.

Schlau, Stacey. "Conformity and Resistance to Enclosure: Female Voices in Rosario Castellanos' *Oficio de tinieblas [The Dark Service]*." *Latin American Literary Review* 12, no. 24 (Spring–Summer 1984): 45–57.

Schmidt, Donald L. "The Indigenista Novel and the Mexican Revolution." *The Americas* 33, no. 4 (April 1977): 652–60.

Schwartz, Kessel. *A New History of Spanish American Fiction.* Coral Gables: University of Miami Press, 1971.

Sommers, Joseph. "The Changing View of the Indian in Mexican Literature." *Hispania* 47, no. 1 (March 1964): 47–55.

———. "The Indian-Oriented Novel in Latin America: New Spirit, New Forms, New Scope." *Journal of Inter-American Studies* 6, no. 1 (1964): 249–65.

———. "Novels of a Dead Revolution." *Nation* 197, no. 6 (1963): 114–15.

Steele, Cynthia. "The Fiction of National Formation: The *Indigenista* Novels of James

Fenimore Cooper and Rosario Castellanos." In *Reinventing the Americas: Comparative Studies of Literature of the United States and Spanish America,* edited by Bell Gale Chevigny and Gari Laguardia, 60–67. New York: Cambridge University Press, 1986.

Stoll, A. K. " 'Arthur Smith salva su alma': Rosario Castellanos and Social Protest." *Crítica Hispánica* 7, no. 2 (1985): 141–47.

Wade, Gerald E., and William H. Archer. "The *Indianista* Novel Since 1889." *Hispania* 33, no. 3 (August 1950): 211–20.

Washington, Thomas. "The Narrative Works of Rosario Castellanos. In Search of History—Confrontations with Myth." Ph.D. diss., University of Minnesota, 1982.

Young, Rinda Rebecca Stowell. "Rosario Castellanos and Elena Garro." In her "Six Representative Women Writers of Mexico, 1960–69," 17–84. Ph.D. diss., University of Illinois, 1975.